COMPREHENSIVE EMOTIONAL INTELLIGENCE

16 Courses

Copyright Page

Title: Comprehensive Emotional Intelligence

Copyright © 2024 by Dr. Jessica Rea Prado

All rights reserved. No part of this publication may be reproduced, distributed, or transmitted in any form or by any means, including photocopying, recording, or other electronic or mechanical methods, without the prior written permission of the publisher, except in the case of brief quotations embodied in critical reviews and certain other noncommercial uses permitted by copyright law.

For permissions requests, write to the author at the address below:

Dr. Jessica Rea Prado: Jessica@Pradoic.com

Cover design by AI, Interior design and typesetting by Jessica Prado and Wayne Brewer

Published by Pradoic, LLC | Pradoic.com

ISBN: 9798344270548

Printed in United States, First Printing: 2024

Disclaimer: The stories and scenarios presented in this book are fictional and intended for educational purposes only. The author and publisher are not responsible for any actions or decisions taken by individuals based on the content of this book. It is recommended that readers seek professional advice or assistance when dealing with real-life situations.

Trademark Notice: Product or corporate names may be trademarks or registered trademarks and are used only for identification and explanation without intent to infringe.

Acknowledgments: The author would like to express gratitude to all the individuals who contributed to the development of this book, including editors, proofreaders, and beta readers. Your insights and support are sincerely appreciated.

Publisher's Note: This book is not intended to substitute for professional advice. The stories and concepts presented here are meant to stimulate thought and discussion but should not be considered a substitute for professional guidance. The reader is encouraged to consult with appropriate professionals regarding their specific situation.

All rights reserved.

About the Author

Dr. Rea Prado has a passion for ability-based emotional intelligence. She is a highly motivated and accomplished professional and possesses a wealth of experience in both corporate and academic settings, with a proven track record of enhancing students' abilities and personal growth leveraging emotional intelligence skills that can be learned at any age. With excellent communication skills and a talent for working effectively with diverse populations, she has excelled across a range of industries. Her ultimate aim is to cultivate emotional intelligence, inspire integrity-driven leadership, and promote genuine collaboration and success in all her endeavors.

Her services are designed to help individuals enhance their emotional intelligence, improve their communication and decision-making skills, and achieve personal and professional success. She offers emotional intelligence facilitation sessions that enable individuals and corporate groups to understand their emotions and those of others and manage them effectively. Her online courses provide comprehensive training on various topics such as effective communication, conflict resolution, and leadership skills. Additionally, her coaching services offer personalized guidance when requested, to support individuals overcoming specific obstacles and achieve their goals.

This book is an encapsulation of her online courses and is often used in conjunction with her corporate training as reference material. For corporate applications, she also offers train-the-trainer versions of the curriculum so that respective human resources teams can leverage her material, and approach, broadly across their organizations on their own, or with her help, customized per situation, for further reinforcement and support.

Learn more about Dr. Rea Prado on her LinkedIn: linkedin.com/in/jessicareaprado or on her website: https://pradoic.info/

Introduction

Welcome to a journey of self-discovery and interpersonal understanding through the lens of Emotional Intelligence (EI). This book, born from a comprehensive curriculum designed for in-depth exploration and practical application, aims to guide you through the multifaceted landscape of emotions and their profound impact on our personal and professional lives.

Emotional Intelligence, once a novel concept, has now emerged as a crucial skill set in navigating the complexities of modern life. It transcends traditional notions of intelligence, encompassing the ability to recognize, understand, manage, and utilize emotions effectively — not just in ourselves, but also in those around us.

This book is structured into 16 courses, mirroring the curriculum that has been successfully implemented in various educational settings. Each chapter delves into a specific aspect of EI, building a comprehensive understanding from the ground up.

We begin by defining Emotional Intelligence and emphasizing its significance in diverse realms of life. From there, we explore the intricacies of understanding and managing our own emotions, a cornerstone of EI. The curriculum progresses to cover the recognition and interpretation of others' emotions, a vital skill in developing empathy and enhancing interpersonal relationships.

Further, the book offers valuable insights into the application of EI in specific contexts like the workplace, where skills like teamwork, leadership, and stress management come to the forefront. The journey through these sessions is not just theoretical; it is replete with practical strategies, exercises, and real-life examples, making the learning experience engaging and applicable.

As you turn the pages, you will find opportunities for reflection, interactive elements, and actionable tips. These are designed not just to impart knowledge, but to encourage a transformational process in your approach to emotions and relationships.

Whether you are a student, an educator, a professional, or simply someone keen on personal growth, this book is your companion in enhancing your Emotional Intelligence. It is a guide to understanding the language of emotions and harnessing that knowledge for better decision-making, relationship building, and self-awareness.

As we embark on this journey together, remember that developing Emotional Intelligence is an ongoing process – one that enriches not just individual lives, but also the fabric of our communities and workplaces. Let us begin this transformative journey towards a more empathetic, understanding, and emotionally intelligent world.

Warm regards,

Dr. Rea Prado

Dr. Rea Prado

Principle Consultant

Pradoic LLC

Table of Contents

Copyright Page	2
About the Author	5
Introduction	7
Table of Contents	9
Thank you	11
Dedication	13

Comprehensive Emotional Intelligence

Learning Objectives for the Comprehensive Curriculum	17
Course 1. Introduction to Emotional Intelligence	19
Course 2. Understanding Emotions	39
Course 3. Emotional Self-Awareness Part 1	55
Course 4. Emotional Self-Awareness Part 2	67
Course 5. Emotional Self-Regulation Part 1	85
Course 6. Emotional Self-Regulation Part 2	103
Course 7. Emotional Self-Regulation Part 3	125
Course 8. Understanding Others' Emotions – Empathy	149
Course 9. Interpersonal Relationships Part 1	171
Course 10. Interpersonal Relationships Part 2	187
Course 11. Interpersonal Relationships Part 3	211

Course 12. Emotional Intelligence in the Workplace Part 1   235

Course 13. Emotional Intelligence in the Workplace Part 2   257

Course 14. Emotional Intelligence in the Workplace Part 3   279

Course 15. Developing Your Emotional Intelligence – Practice and Growth   301

Course 16. Conclusion – Emotional Intelligence in Everyday Life   325

Glossary of Emotional Intelligence Terms   347

Supplemental Book Series Published by Pradoic, LLC   361

Thank you!

Thank you to all of my classmates, professors, and mentors at Adler University. You inspired me during the time I spent in my both master's and PhD curricula. A special thank you to Dr. Samantha Coleman, Dr. Kelli Hogg, Dr. Susan Addams, Dr. Lisa Thomas, and Dr. Cliff Lansley of the Emotional Intelligence Academy.

Dr. Rea Prado

Dedication

I would like to dedicate this book to my friends and family who have supported me through my educational and life journey. And a very special thank you to my favorite person of all time, and one who never doubted my ability to do anything I put my mind to, Zeb Milton Rea, Jr., my beloved grandfather.

- Jessica

Comprehensive Emotional Intelligence

by

Dr. Jessica Rea Prado

Learning Objectives for Comprehensive Emotional Intelligence

---

1. Gain a comprehensive understanding of emotional intelligence, including self-awareness, self-regulation, empathy, and interpersonal skills.

2. Develop techniques for recognizing and managing your own emotions and understanding others' emotions.

3. Understand how to apply emotional intelligence in various contexts, including personal relationships and the workplace.

4. Learn how to handle conflict, stress, and challenges using emotional intelligence techniques.

5. Foster a continuous growth mindset towards developing emotional intelligence skills.

Course 1
Introduction to Emotional Intelligence

Learning Objectives for Course 1

1. Understand the concept and importance of emotional intelligence.

2. Recognize the key components of emotional intelligence.

3. Understand the structure and objectives of the overall curriculum.

Course 1, Section 1
What is Emotional Intelligence?

Emotional Intelligence: Definition

Emotional Intelligence, often abbreviated as EI or EQ (emotional quotient), is the ability to recognize, understand, and manage our own emotions, as well as to recognize, understand, and influence the emotions of others.

First popularized by Daniel Goleman in his 1995 book, "Emotional Intelligence," EI encompasses a broad array of skills and competencies that have significant impacts on personal, academic, and professional success Emotional Intelligence includes:

Self-awareness: This is the ability to understand one's own emotions, strengths, weaknesses, needs, and drives. Self-aware people recognize how their feelings affect them, other people, and their performance. They have a strong understanding of their values and goals and typically are confident in their abilities.

Self-regulation: This involves controlling or redirecting one's disruptive emotions and impulses and adapting to changing circumstances. People who excel in this ability can manage their emotional reactions to all situations and people, even in difficult or stressful situations.

Motivation: People with a high degree of EI are typically motivated by a personal drive to achieve, curiosity about the world, and a love of learning, not just by money or status. They are resilient and optimistic, even in the face of failure.

Empathy: This is the ability to understand the emotional makeup of other people. It's about recognizing and meeting the needs of others and being able to read and respond to the power dynamics in a group or organization.

Social skills: This includes the ability to manage relationships, to build networks, and to understand the dynamics within a group or organization. It involves proficiency in managing relationships and building networks, and an ability to find common ground and build rapport.

Emotional Intelligence: Overview

Emotional Intelligence has been increasingly recognized as an important factor in both personal and professional success. The model of emotional intelligence has evolved over the years, but it broadly covers two main types of competence: Personal competence and social competence.

Personal competence comprises self-awareness and self-management skills, focusing more on the individual than on their interactions with others. Personal competence involves being aware of and regulating one's own emotions, motivating oneself, and recognizing personal strengths and weaknesses.

Social competence consists of social awareness and relationship management skills, involving the ability to understand other people's moods, behaviors, and motives to improve the quality of relationships.

The importance of Emotional Intelligence lies in its impact on various aspects of life:

Personal well-being: Understanding our own emotions can help us navigate our feelings more effectively and maintain a positive state of mind.

Relationships: The ability to comprehend and respond to the feelings of others can lead to better and more fulfilling interpersonal relationships.

Workplace success: EI is crucial for workplace success. It helps in team cooperation, enhances leadership abilities, aids in conflict resolution, and contributes to better decision-making processes.

Academic performance: Research has indicated that students with higher emotional intelligence tend to perform better academically.

Leadership: Emotional intelligence is a crucial part of effective leadership. It allows leaders to connect with their team members, understand their needs and concerns, and respond effectively.

Finally, it's essential to understand that Emotional Intelligence is not static. It can be developed and improved over time with conscious effort, self-reflection, and practice. Therefore, a course in Emotional Intelligence should not only focus on understanding the concept but also on the practical ways in which these skills can be nurtured and applied in daily life.

Course 1, Section 2

Importance of Emotional Intelligence

Why Emotional Intelligence Is Important

Emotional Intelligence is a critical factor that influences various aspects of our lives, ranging from personal well-being to professional success. It touches upon our decision-making processes, our relationships, our stress management, and the way we understand and navigate the world. Here is a comprehensive discussion on why emotional intelligence is crucial in different areas of life.

1. Personal Well-being

Understanding and managing our own emotions plays a significant role in our overall mental health and well-being. High emotional intelligence enables us to identify and express our feelings accurately, thus preventing emotional buildup and stress.

Moreover, emotional intelligence helps individuals become resilient and develop effective coping strategies to manage stressful situations. They can 'bounce back' from adversities faster and more effectively, as they can understand their feelings and quickly adapt to stressful situations.

High emotional intelligence also contributes to increased self-confidence and self-esteem, as it is often associated with a better understanding of one's own strengths and weaknesses. It also enhances other aspects of personal development, such as self-motivation, goal setting, and self-discipline.

2. Relationships

Emotional intelligence is integral to building and maintaining successful relationships, whether it's within a family, between friends, or with a partner.

People with high emotional intelligence are typically better at understanding the emotions and needs of others. They can empathize with others' feelings, which can help in resolving conflicts, enhancing communication, and building stronger bonds.

They can also navigate social networks and read the emotional climate of a group or situation effectively, making them skilled at interpersonal interaction.

Moreover, emotionally intelligent individuals can maintain healthier relationships as they can manage their own emotions well, leading to lesser instances of emotional outbursts or conflicts.

3. Workplace Success

In the professional realm, emotional intelligence is no less critical. It is one of the key factors in fostering a harmonious and productive work environment and is often a distinguishing trait of effective leaders.

Teamwork: Emotional intelligence promotes understanding and empathy within a team, fostering a more collaborative and inclusive work environment. High EI individuals can understand their team members' perspectives, help alleviate tensions, and promote harmonious relationships, leading to increased productivity.

Leadership: Emotionally intelligent leaders can recognize their team members' emotions and are better equipped to respond to their needs. They can motivate their teams, manage stress and conflicts, and foster a positive work environment, enhancing overall team performance. They also often display traits like integrity and authenticity, which can inspire trust and loyalty among team members.

Decision Making: High emotional intelligence can lead to better decision-making, as it fosters an increased understanding of one's own emotions and those of others, enabling a balanced, empathetic approach to decisions.

Conflict Resolution: Emotionally intelligent individuals can effectively navigate and resolve conflicts by understanding and addressing the underlying emotions involved. They can defuse emotionally charged situations and help find mutually acceptable resolutions.

4. Academic Success

While traditionally academic success has been linked with IQ, research has indicated that emotional intelligence can also play a crucial role in academic performance. Emotionally intelligent students are often better at managing stress and can maintain a positive attitude, leading to improved academic performance.

In addition to academic performance, emotional intelligence also contributes to successful social interactions in academic settings. This can lead to more positive relationships with peers and teachers and a more fulfilling educational experience overall.

5. Physical Health

Emotional intelligence can even have an impact on physical health. By understanding our emotions, we can better manage stress and anxiety, which can lead to improved health outcomes. High emotional intelligence can lead to better stress management techniques, resulting in lower blood pressure, a healthier immune system, and overall better physical health.

Conclusion

In conclusion, emotional intelligence touches almost every aspect of our lives. Developing high emotional intelligence can significantly improve personal and professional relationships, academic and workplace success, personal well-being, and even physical health. Therefore, investing time and effort in learning about and improving our emotional intelligence can be highly beneficial. It's not just about understanding emotions; it's about using that understanding to bring about positive outcomes in life.

Course 1, Section 3

Components of Emotional Intelligence

Introduction to the Four Key Components of Emotional Intelligence

Emotional Intelligence, as popularized by Daniel Goleman, can be best understood by examining its four key components: Self-Awareness, Self-Regulation, Empathy, and Interpersonal Skills. These components provide a framework to understand and enhance our capacity to recognize and manage our emotions, as well as those of others. Let's dive deeper into each of these areas:

1. Self-Awareness

Self-awareness forms the foundation of emotional intelligence. It is the ability to recognize and understand one's own emotions as they occur and the way they can affect our thoughts and behavior. Self-aware individuals are mindful of their emotional state and how their emotions can influence their decisions, actions, and relationships.

Understanding one's own emotional strengths, weaknesses, values, and goals also falls under self-awareness. This knowledge provides an understanding of how we come across to others and how we can react to specific situations, which in turn influences our responses and behaviors.

Self-awareness also involves recognizing the relationship between our feelings, what we think, do, and say, as well as our long-term impact on others. People with high self-awareness are usually confident and have a strong sense of self-worth and self-belief, making it easier for them to navigate life's ups and downs.

2. Self-Regulation

Self-regulation, or self-control, refers to our ability to manage our emotions, thoughts, and behaviors in different situations. It involves being able to control emotional impulses, think before acting, and express our emotions in appropriate and constructive ways.

Self-regulation means being able to stay composed and positive even in stressful or difficult situations, and not letting negative emotions or impulses dictate our actions. It also involves an openness to change and the ability to say no to impulsive urges.

People with good self-regulation can manage their stress effectively, stay calm under pressure, and bounce back from setbacks. They can maintain an even keel and are generally flexible and adaptable to changing circumstances.

3. Empathy

Empathy is the ability to understand and share the feelings of others. It is about recognizing others' emotional states and being able to 'put oneself in their shoes.' This component of emotional intelligence helps us form connections with others, allowing us to communicate effectively and maintain good relationships.

Empathy involves more than just being able to understand others' perspectives. It is about recognizing and responding to the needs of others, which is a crucial aspect of effective leadership, teamwork, and interpersonal relations. Empathy leads to compassion and helps behaviors, which build trust and respect.

4. Interpersonal Skills

Interpersonal skills, also referred to as social skills, involve the ability to interact effectively with others. It is about how we use our understanding of our own and others' emotions to manage our relationships, communicate effectively, inspire and influence others, work in teams, and manage conflicts.

Strong interpersonal skills are essential in fostering positive relationships, both personally and professionally. They involve effective verbal and non-verbal communication, active listening, negotiation skills, problem-solving abilities, and the capacity to respect and understand others' perspectives.

Individuals with good interpersonal skills are often excellent team players. They can manage relationships and build networks, and they have the ability to find common ground and build rapport. They are also effective at leading, persuading, and influencing others, resolving conflicts constructively, and providing and receiving feedback effectively.

Conclusion

In essence, these four components of emotional intelligence are interconnected and contribute to our ability to navigate our emotional world effectively. They help us understand ourselves and others better, improve our reactions to emotional situations, foster fulfilling relationships, and lead a balanced, emotionally healthy life. Developing these components can significantly improve our emotional intelligence and contribute to personal and professional success.

Course 1, Section 4

Course Structure and Objectives

1. Introduction to Emotional Intelligence

    a. Understand the concept and importance of emotional intelligence.

    b. Recognize the key components of emotional intelligence.

    c. Understand the structure and objectives of the whole curriculum.

2. Understanding Emotions

    a. Understand the basic concept of what emotions are & why they matter.

    b. Recognize how emotions work, including how they are triggered and processed.

    c. Understand the role and influence of emotions in our daily lives.

3. Emotional Self-Awareness Part 1

    a. Understand the concept of emotional self-awareness.

    b. Develop the ability to recognize and name one's own emotions accurately.

    c. Understand the benefits of emotional self-awareness and how it influences our responses and interactions.

4. Emotional Self-Awareness Part 2

a. Learn what emotional triggers are and how they impact our emotional state.

b. Gain strategies for identifying personal emotional triggers.

c. Understand the significance of emotional self-awareness in personal growth and relationships.

5. Emotional Self-Regulation Part 1

a. Deepen the understanding of emotional triggers and their impacts.

b. Learn practical techniques for responding to emotional triggers in a healthier way.

c. Explore the process of self-regulation and its role in managing emotional triggers.

6. Emotional Self-Regulation Part 2

a. Understand the concepts of self-soothing and calming techniques and their importance in emotional self-regulation.

b. Learn a range of practical techniques for calming and soothing oneself when faced with strong or negative emotions.

c. Apply these techniques in practice scenarios and daily life.

7. Emotional Self-Regulation Part 3

a. Understand the concept of cognitive reappraisal and its importance in emotional regulation.

b. Learn about cognitive distortions and how they affect our emotional responses.

c. Master techniques for cognitive reappraisal and handling intense emotions.

d. Apply these strategies in real-life scenarios and daily life.

8. Understanding Others' Emotions – Empathy

    a. Understand the concept of empathy & its role in emotional intelligence.

    b. Learn to recognize and identify others' emotions effectively.

    c. Master techniques for empathetic listening and response.

    d. Apply these strategies in real-life interactions and relationships.

9. Interpersonal Relationships Part 1

    a. Understand the role of emotional intelligence in communication and conflict management.

    b. Learn the techniques of effective communication and how to apply them in personal and professional relationships.

    c. Understand the concept of conflict, its sources, and the role of emotions in conflict situations.

    d. Learn the techniques of conflict management and resolution, focusing on emotional intelligence strategies.

10. Interpersonal Relationships Part 2

    a. Understand the role of emotional intelligence in setting and maintaining healthy boundaries in relationships.

    b. Learn techniques for setting boundaries and saying no respectfully and assertively.

    c. Understand the challenges of dealing with difficult people and how emotional intelligence can help navigate these situations.

    d. Learn strategies for dealing with various types of difficult people.

11. Interpersonal Relationships Part 3

a. Understand how emotional intelligence can guide us in complex social situations.

b. Learn techniques for navigating intricate social contexts, like workplace politics, multicultural environments, or challenging family dynamics.

c. Understand the role of emotional intelligence in maintaining healthy relationships over time.

d. Learn strategies for maintaining relationship health, such as regular check-ins, active listening, and expressing appreciation.

12. Emotional Intelligence in the Workplace – Part 1

a. Understand the role of emotional intelligence in teamwork and collaboration within a workplace setting.

b. Learn techniques to enhance teamwork through emotional intelligence, such as empathetic communication and effective conflict resolution.

c. Recognize the benefits of emotionally intelligent teamwork to individual and organizational success.

13. Emotional Intelligence in the Workplace – Part 2

a. Understand the role of emotional intelligence in effective leadership and influence.

b. Learn how to leverage emotional intelligence to build influence in the workplace.

c. Develop strategies for leading with emotional intelligence.

14. Emotional Intelligence in the Workplace – Part 3

a. Understand the role of emotional intelligence in managing workplace stress and preventing burnout.

b. Learn strategies to manage stress and prevent burnout using emotional intelligence.

c. Apply emotional intelligence skills in practical scenarios to manage stress and prevent burnout.

15. Developing Your Emotional Intelligence – Practice and Growth

a. Understand the importance of ongoing practice and growth in emotional intelligence.

b. Learn about strategies and exercises that support the continued development of emotional intelligence.

c. Apply emotional intelligence strategies and exercises in daily life.

16. Conclusion – Emotional Intelligence in Everyday Life

a. Review and summarize key points from the entire course.

b. Understand the applications of emotional intelligence in everyday life.

c. Reflect on personal growth throughout the course and plan for the journey ahead.

Supplementary Material

A Story of Emotional Intelligence

The Turning Point

Olivia Jennings was an executive admired for her technical acumen. She could outpace anyone in her field, and her unwavering competence was known throughout the industry. Yet, despite her individual prowess, Olivia was blind to a glaring issue: her team's morale was flagging, their performance declining, and their unity slowly fragmenting.

The realization came abruptly during her annual performance review. Her supervisor gently pointed out, "Olivia, your technical expertise is unparalleled, but it seems like your team isn't performing at its best. I think it might be due to a lack of connection between you and the team."

Olivia was taken aback. She hadn't realized that there was a problem. She thought her team was just as driven and motivated as she was. After the meeting, she reflected on her interactions with her team. She realized that while she had been adept at solving technical problems and reaching project deadlines, she hadn't truly connected with her team on a deeper level.

It was a wake-up call for Olivia. She knew something had to change, so she embarked on a journey of self-improvement, hoping to develop what she later learned was known as emotional intelligence.

The journey began with understanding her own emotions – recognizing when she was stressed or frustrated, understanding what caused these emotions, and how they influenced her reactions. This self-awareness was a revelation. She realized that her often brusque manner, which she thought was just her being focused, could come across as cold or unapproachable to her team.

Next came self-regulation. Olivia learned to pause and take a deep breath before reacting to a stressful situation. She found that this momentary break allowed her to respond more thoughtfully, reducing unnecessary conflicts and misunderstandings.

The learning of empathy was a game-changer for Olivia. She made a conscious effort to listen to her team's ideas, concerns, and feelings. She encouraged open communication and made an effort to understand things from their perspectives.

This shift resulted in the team feeling valued and heard, which greatly improved their morale.

Finally, she worked on her interpersonal skills. She made an effort to communicate more effectively, providing clear direction and expectations, while also fostering a collaborative environment. She also improved her conflict resolution skills, ensuring disagreements were addressed constructively, preserving the team's unity.

Over time, the changes in Olivia were palpable. She was no longer just the 'taskmaster' but also a mentor, guide, and most importantly, a leader who could unite her team. The atmosphere changed from one of silent endurance to one of enthusiastic cooperation. Her team's performance began to improve, not just in terms of output, but also in creativity and initiative. They were more engaged, and it was clear they felt a greater sense of belonging.

"The Turning Point" highlights the journey of Olivia as she learns about and embraces emotional intelligence. This narrative is a testament to the importance of emotional intelligence, demonstrating its impact on personal growth, team performance, and organizational success. It sets the stage for the comprehensive curriculum that follows, each part of which aims to explore various aspects of emotional intelligence and its application, similar to Olivia's journey.

Summary

This course will provide learners with the tools to understand and improve their emotional intelligence. By exploring emotions and their triggers, practicing self-awareness and regulation, understanding empathy and interpersonal relationships, and applying these skills in various social and professional contexts, students will be able to navigate their emotional world more effectively. The goal is for students to emerge with a heightened sense of emotional intelligence, ready to engage more positively with themselves and those around them, just like Olivia.

Course 2
Understanding Emotions

Learning Objectives for Course 2

1. Understand the basic concept of what emotions are & why they matter.

2. Recognize how emotions work, including how they are triggered and processed.

3. Understand the role and influence of emotions in our daily lives.

Course 2, Section 1

What are Emotions?

Understanding Emotions: The Colorful Spectrum of Human Experience

Emotions play a crucial role in our lives, influencing our decisions, shaping our behaviors, and coloring our perceptions. They are complex psychological and physiological responses that arise as we interact with our environment and internal thoughts. These reactions, though often automatic and unconscious, have profound implications on our mental and physical well-being.

The range of emotions we experience is broad and varies in intensity. From subtle shifts in mood to potent feelings that can overwhelm us, our emotions form a dynamic, ever-changing landscape.

At the most fundamental level, there are several basic or primary emotions that are recognized universally across cultures:

1. **Happiness**: A positive emotion characterized by contentment, satisfaction, or joy. Happiness often arises when we experience success, pleasure, or a sense of connection with others.

2. **Sadness**: A negative emotion often associated with loss, disappointment, or perceived failure. It's a natural response to situations that are hurtful, and it may lead us to seek comfort or withdraw to heal.

3. **Fear**: An intense emotion triggered by perceived danger or threat; fear's primary function is to protect us from harm. It prepares the body for a fight or flight response.

4. **Disgust**: This emotion arises as a response to something offensive or repulsive. Disgust can protect us from harmful substances or behaviors, guiding us away from what could potentially harm us.

5. **Anger**: A strong negative emotion usually triggered by perceived unfairness, threats, or violations. Anger can energize us to confront or address issues but can also lead to conflict if not managed properly.

6. **Surprise**: A sudden emotional response to unexpected events. Surprises can be positive or negative depending on the nature of the unexpected situation.

While these basic emotions are experienced universally, there are many more complex or secondary emotions that we can experience as humans. These often arise from combinations of primary emotions or as nuanced responses to specific situations. They include feelings such as:

1. **Anticipation**: A feeling of excitement or anxiety about what is to come. It can be positive, as in looking forward to a vacation, or negative, such as fearing an upcoming exam.

2. **Trust**: A positive emotion resulting from reliance or confidence in the reliability, truth, or strength of someone or something.

3. **Shame**: A painful emotion experienced as a response to something regrettable or dishonorable done by oneself.

4. **Guilt**: Similar to shame, guilt is associated with feeling remorse for one's actions, particularly those that are perceived as wrong or harmful to others.

5. **Envy**: A complex emotion involving feeling discontented or resentful because of someone else's possessions, qualities, or luck.

6. **Pride**: A positive emotion that stems from a personal achievement or the achievements of those we care about.

7. **Contempt**: A complex emotion that often arises from feelings of disrespect or disdain towards someone or something.

Understanding the range of emotions is the first step towards emotional intelligence. Emotions are not inherently 'good' or 'bad'; they simply are signals that inform us about our current state and how we are interpreting our environment. By learning to recognize and understand our emotions, we can better manage them and use them as tools for personal growth, enhanced relationships, and overall well-being. Our emotional landscape is a rich and colorful spectrum, and each emotion, whether comfortable or not, has a valuable role to play.

A lot of good work has been done in the area of defining and categorizing emotions. The emotions listed above are the primary ones used in this course to provide the foundations of emotional intelligence. Much more information can be found from great researchers on this topic such as Gloria Wilcox.

Reference Material: Gloria Willcox (1982) The Feeling Wheel, Transactional Analysis Journal, 12:4, 274-276, DOI: 10.1177/036215378201200411

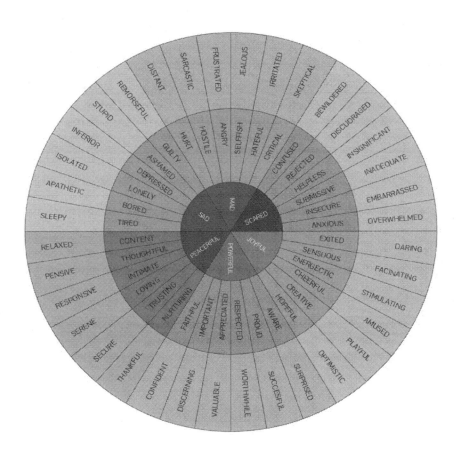

Course 2, Section 2
The Origin and Purpose of Emotions

Emotions: The Evolutionary Compass Guiding Human Behavior

Emotions have always been an integral part of human survival and evolution. From our ancient ancestors who roamed the savannah to modern humans navigating complex social networks, emotions have served as an internal compass, guiding our actions, influencing our decisions, and shaping our interactions.

To understand the evolutionary purpose of emotions, let's take a step back and consider the basic function of any living organism: survival and reproduction. In this context, emotions can be seen as evolution's solution to the problem of how to make quick and effective decisions that optimize chances for survival and reproduction.

Survival

Emotions serve as our body's immediate response system. They arise in response to stimuli from our environment and provide us with a quick, automated way to react that doesn't require conscious thought.

For instance, the emotion of fear prepares our body for immediate action when we perceive danger or threat. The physical sensations associated with fear, such as a faster heart rate, quickened breathing, or heightened senses, are all part of our body's "fight or flight" response. This response equips us to either confront the danger (fight) or escape from it (flight). Therefore, fear plays a crucial role in protecting us from harm.

Similarly, the emotion of disgust evolved to protect us from harmful substances or pathogens. The strong aversion and physiological response (like nausea) we experience when confronted with rotten food, for example, help us avoid potential sources of disease.

Reproduction and Social Cohesion

Apart from survival, emotions also serve an important function in our social lives. As social animals, humans rely on cooperation and cohesion within groups for survival.

Emotions facilitate these social bonds and enable us to navigate complex social dynamics.

Consider the emotion of love, for instance. The powerful feelings of attachment and desire associated with love encourage long-term pair bonding, which can lead to better care for offspring, increasing their survival rates. Similarly, the feelings of joy and happiness that come from social interaction and cooperation encourage us to engage in these behaviors, strengthening social bonds and promoting group cohesion.

Emotions like guilt and shame also play a significant role in maintaining social order. They arise when we violate social norms or ethics and motivate us to rectify our wrongs, apologize, or make amends. By experiencing guilt or shame, we are discouraged from repeating behaviors that could harm our social standing or relationships.

Emotions as Communication

Lastly, emotions also serve as a form of non-verbal communication. Emotional expressions are universally recognized across cultures, suggesting they are an inherent part of our human biology. When we feel scared, happy, or surprised, the changes in our facial expressions, body language, and tone of voice can convey these feelings to others around us. This communication can help others understand our needs, responses, or intentions, enabling more effective social interaction.

Moreover, perceiving and responding to the emotions of others is a fundamental aspect of empathy, a skill crucial for social cohesion and cooperation. By understanding and sharing the feelings of others, we can better support and cooperate with each other, further enhancing our chances of survival and reproductive success.

In conclusion, emotions have evolved to play a significant role in our survival, reproduction, and social interactions. They guide our behaviors, decisions, and communication, helping us navigate the world effectively. As we journey towards emotional intelligence, understanding the evolutionary purpose of emotions provides a broader context for why we feel the way we do and how these feelings influence our lives.

Course 2, Section 3

How Emotions Work

The Process of Emotional Experience: From Trigger to Conscious Recognition

Understanding the process of how emotions are triggered, experienced, and managed is a crucial component in the journey of emotional intelligence. This process involves a complex interplay between our environment, our brain, and our body, leading to the conscious experience and management of emotions. Let's take a deeper look at each of these steps.

1. Emotional Trigger

The process of emotional experience starts with a trigger. This can be an external event, like receiving good news, a hostile interaction, or seeing a loved one in danger. It could also be internal, such as a memory or thought that evokes a strong emotional response. The trigger is essentially any stimulus that elicits an emotional response.

2. Perception and Appraisal

Once the trigger is present, our brain perceives and appraises the situation. This evaluation happens in fractions of a second and is often unconscious. The brain evaluates whether the trigger is a threat, a reward, a loss, or something else. This appraisal is influenced by a multitude of factors, such as past experiences, our current state of mind, and our individual beliefs and values.

The appraisal process primarily takes place in the amygdala, a small, almond-shaped structure in our brain that's instrumental in emotion processing. The amygdala receives inputs from our senses and other brain regions and quickly assesses the emotional significance of the situation.

3. Physiological Response

Following the appraisal, our brain initiates a physiological response, preparing the body to respond appropriately. This is coordinated by the autonomic nervous system, which controls involuntary bodily functions.

In response to a perceived threat, for example, the sympathetic branch of the autonomic nervous system initiates the "fight or flight" response. This involves physiological changes like increased heart rate, rapid breathing, dilated pupils, and a rush of adrenaline. These changes prime the body for action, either to confront the threat (fight) or flee from it (flight).

Alternatively, if the appraisal leads to a positive emotion like happiness, the body may relax, with the parasympathetic branch of the autonomic nervous system calming bodily functions, reducing heart rate and breathing, and promoting restful processes.

4. Emotional Experience

The physiological changes accompanying an emotion don't usually happen in isolation; they're accompanied by the subjective, conscious experience of emotion. This is what we commonly refer to when we say we're "feeling" an emotion.

This conscious experience is thought to arise from the combination of the physiological response and the way our brain interprets this response based on the original appraisal. This emotional experience is highly personal and subjective. Two people can experience the same situation, yet feel different emotions, because their brains may appraise the situation differently based on their individual perspectives, experiences, and contexts.

5. Expression of Emotion

Emotions are often accompanied by observable expressions. These can include facial expressions, body language, and changes in the tone of voice. Expressing emotions is a form of non-verbal communication and plays a critical role in social interactions, helping us convey our feelings, intentions, or needs to others.

6. Regulation of Emotion

Emotion regulation is the process by which we influence which emotions we have, when we have them, and how we experience and express them. This could mean intensifying, reducing, or maintaining the intensity or duration of a particular emotion.

Emotion regulation strategies can be conscious and deliberate, like using cognitive reappraisal (reinterpreting an emotion-eliciting situation in a way that changes its emotional impact), or they can be unconscious and automatic, like distraction or suppression.

Conclusion

In summary, the process of experiencing an emotion involves a sequence of events: an emotional trigger leads to an appraisal, which initiates a physiological response. This response, combined with our cognitive interpretation, leads to the conscious experience of emotion. We express our emotions and, finally, manage or regulate them. Understanding this process is crucial for developing emotional intelligence, as it provides a foundation for recognizing and effectively managing our emotional experiences.

Course 2, Section 4

The Role and Influence of Emotions in Our Lives

Emotions and Decision Making

Emotions significantly influence our decision-making processes. They provide us with important information about our environment and help us evaluate options and make decisions quickly. This is particularly true when the information is ambiguous, or the decisions are complex. The emotional value attached to outcomes and choices plays a key role in guiding our decisions.

However, emotions can also lead us astray if we rely on them too much or don't consider them enough. For example, feeling anxious can lead to an overly cautious approach, while feeling overly optimistic can result in rash, under-thought decisions. Emotional intelligence involves learning to incorporate emotions appropriately into decision making, balancing emotional input with logical reasoning.

Emotions and Behavior

Our emotions directly influence our behavior. They can motivate us to take action, discourage us from engaging in certain activities, and change the intensity or frequency of our behaviors. For instance, fear can prompt us to avoid potentially harmful situations, while joy can encourage us to seek out and repeat pleasurable experiences. Anger can stimulate confrontational or aggressive behaviors, while sadness can lead to withdrawal and isolation. Emotional intelligence involves recognizing and managing these emotional drivers of behavior to promote more adaptive responses.

Emotions and Relationships

Emotions play a vital role in our relationships. They are essential for social bonding, expressing empathy, and navigating social interactions. Positive emotions like love, joy, and gratitude can foster closeness and intimacy, while negative emotions like anger, jealousy, or resentment can cause conflicts and distance.

Emotionally intelligent individuals can read and respond to others' emotions effectively, which can enhance their relationships. They're also able to manage their own emotions in a relationship context, helping to prevent negative emotions from leading to destructive behaviors. They're also better at repairing relational issues when they do occur, by expressing and managing emotions constructively.

Emotions and Well-being

Our emotions have a profound impact on our psychological and physical well-being. Chronic exposure to stress and negative emotions can lead to mental health issues like depression and anxiety, and physical health problems like heart disease and a weakened immune system. On the other hand, positive emotions have been linked to better mental and physical health, longer lifespan, and higher quality of life.

Emotional intelligence helps in managing both positive and negative emotions for improved well-being. It encourages the cultivation and prolonging of positive emotional experiences and provides tools to navigate and recover from negative emotional experiences more effectively. It can also enable us to seek help and support when needed, further enhancing our well-being.

In summary, emotions significantly influence our decision-making, behaviors, relationships, and overall well-being. Emotional intelligence, therefore, provides a crucial toolkit for managing these areas of life, helping us to make better decisions, engage in adaptive behaviors, enhance our relationships, and improve our overall well-being.

Supplementary Material: Emotional Intelligence Perspectives

The Tale of Two Reactions

Carlos and DeAndre had been waiting eagerly for the annual summer music festival. It was their yearly tradition, a time to let loose, dance, and revel in the melodies of their favorite bands. They had been looking forward to it for months, so the announcement that it was canceled due to unforeseen circumstances hit them hard. But their reactions to the disappointing news couldn't have been more different.

When Carlos saw the cancellation notice on his phone, he was overcome with anger. His heart pounded in his chest as he thought about the vacation days he'd taken from work, the new tent he'd bought, and all the plans that were suddenly ruined. He slammed his hand on the table, startling DeAndre who was sitting across from him.

"That's just great! The one thing I was looking forward to this whole year, and it's canceled," he spat, his voice heavy with bitterness. Carlos's whole day spiraled downwards from there. He was snappy with his coworkers, snapped at a barista over a minor mix-up with his coffee order, and ended the day with a throbbing headache and a sense of frustration.

DeAndre, on the other hand, took a deep breath when he read the news. His stomach churned with disappointment, and he could feel the DeAndre surge of anger that Carlos had expressed. But instead of lashing out, he allowed himself a moment to feel the disappointment, acknowledging it was okay to feel upset about something he'd been looking forward to.

Rather than letting the disappointment ruin his day, he started thinking of other ways they could still make the most of their time off. After all, they still had vacation days, and the new tent could still be put to use.

"Hey, I know it's a bummer about the festival," DeAndre said, trying to catch Carlos's eye. "But why don't we have our own music festival? We could drive up to the lake, camp out, and bring along some of our favorite music. It wouldn't be the DeAndre, but it could still be fun."

At first, Carlos was resistant. But as he watched DeAndre continue with his day, handling disappointments without letting them ruin his mood, he began to reflect. He thought about the anger that had consumed him and how it had affected his day. And he compared it to DeAndre's response, who had managed to turn the situation around by processing his disappointment differently.

In the end, Carlos admitted that DeAndre had the right idea. They planned their own 'lake festival', inviting a few friends, and packing their cars with camping gear and speakers. It turned out to be one of the best weekends they'd ever had, filled with laughter, campfires, and dancing under the stars.

Conclusion

"The Tale of Two Reactions" highlights the importance of understanding our emotions. Both Carlos and DeAndre experienced disappointment, but their reactions determined the course of their day and ultimately their experience. Through understanding and managing our emotions effectively, we can navigate life's disappointments constructively, turning potential frustrations into opportunities for growth and positivity.

Course 3
Emotional Self-Awareness Part 1
Recognizing and Naming Our Emotions

Learning Objectives for Course 3

1. Understand the concept of emotional self-awareness.

2. Develop the ability to recognize and name one's own emotions accurately.

3. Understand the benefits of emotional self-awareness and how it influences our responses and interactions.

Course 3, Section 1

Introduction to Emotional Self-Awareness

Emotional Self-Awareness

Emotional self-awareness, a fundamental aspect of emotional intelligence, refers to the ability to recognize and understand one's own emotions. It is the capacity to identify and name our emotional states accurately and to understand the links between our feelings, thoughts, and behaviors.

When we talk about recognizing and naming our emotions, we refer to the ability to observe our emotional state and describe it accurately. This can range from basic emotions, such as happiness, sadness, anger, surprise, fear, and disgust, to more complex feelings, such as disappointment, anxiety, excitement, embarrassment, or contentment. It's important to be as specific as possible in identifying these emotions as each feeling can guide us differently in how we react or respond to situations.

The importance of emotional self-awareness cannot be overstated. Here's why:

1. **Improved Understanding of Self**: Being emotionally self-aware means understanding what we are feeling and why. This awareness can provide valuable insights into understanding our strengths, weaknesses, thoughts, beliefs, motivations, and values.

2. **Better Decision-Making**: Our emotions can significantly influence our decision-making process. By being aware of how we're feeling, we can better understand how our emotions might be swaying our choices and actions, enabling us to make more balanced, thoughtful decisions.

3. **Enhanced Self-Regulation**: Understanding our emotional states can help us to manage our emotional responses better. If we can identify our emotions accurately, we can apply strategies to cope with them more effectively, whether that means calming ourselves down when we're angry or finding ways to lift our spirits when we're sad.

4. **Healthier Relationships**: Emotional self-awareness can improve our relationships. By understanding our emotions, we're better equipped to express our feelings and

needs effectively. Additionally, being aware of our emotional state can help us understand others' emotions, fostering empathy, and understanding.

5. **Increased Self-Confidence**: When we understand our emotions, we feel more in control. This understanding fosters confidence because we are less likely to be caught off guard by our emotional responses.

Conclusion

In summary, emotional self-awareness is a critical first step in developing emotional intelligence. It forms the foundation upon which other emotional skills are built, including emotional regulation, empathy, and interpersonal skills. As we dive deeper into the topic, we'll explore various techniques to enhance our emotional self-awareness, making it a robust tool in our emotional intelligence toolkit.

Course 3, Section 2: Recognizing Emotions
The First Step in Emotional Self-Awareness

Recognizing Emotions: The First Step in Emotional Self-Awareness

Recognizing our emotions is indeed the first, crucial step in developing emotional self-awareness. By identifying what we are feeling at any given moment, we start the process of understanding our emotional landscape and how it influences our thoughts, decisions, and behaviors.

Human beings can experience a wide range of emotions. These can range from basic emotions such as happiness, sadness, fear, anger, surprise, and disgust to more nuanced emotions such as embarrassment, guilt, pride, shame, elation, and many others. Each emotion is a unique blend of thoughts, physical sensations, and behavioral responses.

The recognition of emotions goes beyond merely labeling them. It involves observing the interplay between our thoughts, physical sensations, and behaviors associated with each emotion. For instance, anger might come with heated thoughts of injustice, a rapid heart rate, and a desire to lash out or defend oneself. Recognizing these patterns helps us identify our emotional state accurately and gives us essential information about how we might want to respond.

Consider two real-life examples:

1. **Anna at work**: Anna is a project manager who's just been informed that her team's project deadline has been moved up by a week. She feels her heart racing, notices tension in her jaw and experiences a flurry of thoughts around the unfairness of the situation and the stress it will cause her team. Recognizing these signs, Anna identifies that she's feeling a mix of anger and anxiety. This recognition allows her to pause and choose how to respond rather than reacting impulsively out of anger or fear.

2. **Ben at home**: Ben's friend just canceled their weekend plans at the last minute. He feels a sinking feeling in his stomach, a heaviness in his chest, and thoughts of disappointment. By recognizing these sensations and thoughts, Ben identifies that

he's feeling disappointed and hurt. This awareness allows him to express his feelings to his friend in a constructive conversation about reliability and respect in their friendship.

Conclusion

The process of recognizing emotions can be challenging due to the variety and complexity of emotions we experience. It's common for people to experience multiple emotions simultaneously, or for one emotion to quickly shift into another. For example, disappointment can turn into resentment, or fear can shift into relief.

Benefits

Despite these complexities, the ability to recognize emotions brings many benefits:

> 1. **Better Emotional Management**: Recognizing an emotion is the first step in managing it. Only when we know what we're feeling can we choose an appropriate response.
>
> 2. **Improved Decision Making**: Our emotions can significantly influence our decisions. By recognizing what we're feeling, we can take a step back and ensure our decisions are rational and beneficial, rather than impulsive or emotion driven.
>
> 3. **Enhanced Communication**: Recognizing our emotions allows us to communicate our feelings accurately to others, fostering better understanding and cooperation.
>
> 4. **Greater Empathy**: By learning to recognize our emotions, we become better at recognizing emotions in others, leading to greater empathy and better interpersonal relationships.

Conclusion

In conclusion, the process of recognizing emotions, while complex, plays a crucial role in emotional self-awareness and broader emotional intelligence. This skill is the steppingstone to understanding ourselves better and navigating our personal and professional lives more effectively.

Course 3, Section 3
How to Identify and Name Emotions

How to Identify and Name Emotions

The ability to accurately identify and name our emotions is a vital skill in emotional self-awareness. Although it may seem challenging, especially for complex or nuanced emotions, several practical steps and techniques can help us get better at this. Here's how:

1. **Introspection**: The first step to identifying emotions is taking the time to introspect. When you notice an emotional response, pause and turn your attention inward. Ask yourself, "What am I feeling right now?" Try to step back and observe your emotional state without judgment or rush to action.

2. **Body Scan Meditation**: Our bodies often give clues about our emotional state. Body scan meditation is a mindfulness technique that helps tune into these physical sensations. To do this, find a quiet space, close your eyes, and take a few deep breaths. Then, mentally scan your body from head to toe, noting any tension, discomfort, or other sensations. For instance, you might notice a tightness in your chest when you're anxious or a fluttery stomach when you're excited. Associating these physical sensations with specific emotions can help you identify your feelings more accurately.

3. **Emotional Vocabulary Expansion**: Sometimes, we struggle to identify our emotions because we lack the vocabulary to describe them. Expanding your emotional vocabulary can help. Look up "emotion words" or "feelings list" online and familiarize yourself with a broader range of emotions. You might discover more accurate descriptors for your feelings, like "frustrated" instead of just "mad," or "content" instead of just "okay."

4. **Emotional Journaling**: Writing about your emotions can provide clarity and insight. Try to make a habit of journaling about your day, focusing especially on your emotional experiences. Write down what happened, how you felt, and any thoughts or physical sensations associated with these emotions. Over time, this practice can help you get better at recognizing and naming your feelings.

5. **The Feeling Wheel**: The Feeling Wheel, developed by Dr. Gloria Willcox, is a useful tool for identifying and naming emotions. The wheel is organized with six primary emotions at the center: happy, sad, scared, mad, surprised, and peaceful. Each of these emotions branches out into more nuanced emotions. By identifying the primary emotion first, you can then move outward on the wheel to find more specific emotions you might be experiencing. (See Course 2, Section 1 for the graphic)

6. **Mindfulness Practice**: Mindfulness is the practice of being fully present and engaged in the current moment, non-judgmentally. Regular mindfulness practice, such as daily meditation or mindful breathing exercises, can increase your awareness of your emotions as they arise, making it easier to identify and name them.

7. **Seek Feedback**: Sometimes, an outside perspective can be helpful. Discuss your emotional experiences with trusted friends, family, or a mental health professional. They might provide insights that help you better identify and name your emotions.

8. **Use Artistic Expression**: Sometimes, emotions are hard to put into words. Artistic expressions such as drawing, painting, dancing, or making music can help you express and identify your emotions.

Conclusion

Remember, like any other skill, recognizing and naming emotions takes practice. You might not always get it right, and that's okay. The goal is not perfection but a better understanding of your emotional world. The more you practice, the more intuitive and effective this process will become, contributing significantly to your emotional self-awareness and overall emotional intelligence.

Course 3, Section 4

The Benefits of Emotional Self-Awareness

The Benefits of Emotional Self-Awareness

Emotional self-awareness is a foundational skill in emotional intelligence, and it brings several benefits that enhance various aspects of our lives. This skill not only promotes personal growth but also positively impacts our decision-making, stress management, and interpersonal relationships, among others. Let's dive deeper into these benefits:

1. **Improved Decision-Making**: Our emotions often influence our decisions, whether we realize it or not. For example, we might make impulsive decisions when we're angry or overly cautious ones when we're afraid. Emotional self-awareness allows us to recognize these emotional influences and factor them into our decision-making processes. By understanding our emotional responses, we can make more informed, balanced decisions rather than being swayed by transient emotional states.

2. **Better Stress Management**: Stress is often linked to our emotional responses to challenging or overwhelming situations. With emotional self-awareness, we can notice when our stress levels are rising and understand what's causing this stress. This awareness allows us to address the stressor directly or use stress management techniques effectively. Recognizing emotions like anxiety or worry early on can prevent these feelings from escalating into full-blown stress or panic.

3. **Enhanced Relationships**: Emotional self-awareness also plays a critical role in our relationships. When we understand our emotions, we can express them more clearly and constructively, leading to better communication. This awareness can also help us understand and navigate conflicts better. For example, recognizing that you're feeling defensive can help you step back, calm down, and address the issue more effectively. By managing our emotions effectively, we can nurture healthier, more fulfilling relationships.

4. **Greater Self-Control**: By recognizing our emotions as they arise, we can respond to them proactively rather than reactively. If we're aware that we're becoming angry, for instance, we can take steps to cool down before we say or do something

we might regret later. This kind of self-control is crucial in many areas of life, including work, relationships, and personal well-being.

5. **Personal Growth and Self-Understanding**: Emotional self-awareness is key to personal growth. By understanding our emotional patterns, we can identify areas for improvement, such as emotional triggers that consistently lead to negative feelings or reactions. Emotional self-awareness can also help us understand what we need to feel happy, fulfilled, and emotionally balanced.

6. **Increased Empathy and Compassion**: Understanding our emotions can help us empathize with others' emotions, fostering a deeper connection and understanding with those around us. It also allows us to have greater compassion for ourselves when we experience negative emotions. Rather than being harsh or judgmental towards us, we can recognize that it's natural to have a wide range of feelings.

7. **Better Performance at Work**: In the workplace, emotional self-awareness can lead to better performance. Being aware of your emotions allows you to manage them effectively, reducing the risk of unproductive emotional responses disrupting your work. It can also make you more attuned to the feelings of your coworkers, fostering better teamwork, communication, and overall work environment.

Conclusion

In conclusion, emotional self-awareness brings numerous benefits that touch all aspects of our lives. It's not always an easy skill to cultivate, but the rewards are well worth the effort. As we continue this journey of emotional intelligence, we will delve into more practical strategies to enhance emotional self-awareness and reap these benefits.

Supplementary Material: Everyday Emotional Intelligence

A Day in the Life of Alex

It was a Tuesday morning, and Alex's alarm blared at 6:30 a.m., jolting him awake. Alex lay in bed, groggy and disoriented, his heart pounding in response to the sudden awakening. He recognized the irritation stirring in him, and instead of hitting snooze and going back to sleep, he took a moment to acknowledge his feeling: "I'm irritated because the alarm was too loud."

Acknowledging his irritation, Alex decided to adjust the alarm volume later in the day to avoid the same experience the following morning. He climbed out of bed and went about his morning routine, appreciating his small act of emotional self-awareness and regulation.

While having breakfast, Alex checked his emails and noticed one from his boss, requesting a detailed report by the end of the day. An immediate rush of anxiety flooded him. Instead of panicking, Alex took a moment to recognize his emotion. "I am feeling anxious because this report will require a lot of work and time," he named it.

Realizing the source of his anxiety, Alex took a few deep breaths, calming his racing heart. He decided to plan his day around this task, prioritizing it over less pressing duties. His emotional self-awareness had helped him to manage his reaction effectively, reducing his anxiety and helping him come up with a productive strategy.

At work, during a team meeting, Alex found himself feeling frustrated as a colleague continually interrupted him while he was speaking. Instead of reacting sharply, as he might have in the past, he identified his emotion: "I am frustrated because I'm being interrupted and not being heard." After the meeting, Alex decided to talk to his colleague about it privately. His conversation was open, calm, and respectful, leading to a positive resolution - his colleague apologized and promised to be more conscious of giving everyone a chance to speak.

Later in the afternoon, Alex started to feel tired and noticed a dip in his productivity. He felt a sense of guilt creeping in for not working at his usual pace. Identifying his emotion, Alex thought, "I'm feeling guilty because I believe I'm not being productive enough." He acknowledged that it's normal to have productivity fluctuations and reminded himself that pushing through fatigue often leads to more mistakes and lower quality work. So, he took a short break, took a walk outside to refresh himself, and returned to his work with renewed energy.

In the evening, Alex met with some friends for dinner. He found himself feeling unusually quiet and detached from the lively conversation around him. Instead of dismissing his feelings, he recognized and named it: "I'm feeling withdrawn because I'm still processing the events of my day." Recognizing his need for some quiet time, he excused himself early from the dinner and spent some time alone, reflecting on his day.

As he prepared for bed, Alex acknowledged the range of emotions he'd experienced throughout his day - irritation, anxiety, frustration, guilt, and withdrawal. Recognizing and naming these emotions allowed him to navigate his day more effectively, and he could see the positive impacts it had on his actions, decisions, and interactions.

As he turned off the lights, he felt a sense of accomplishment. His day hadn't been perfect, but he'd successfully practiced emotional self-awareness and, in doing so, had created a blueprint for better managing his emotions in the future. Feeling grateful for the progress he'd made, Alex drifted off to sleep, ready to face another day with increased emotional self-awareness.

What's Next…

This course sets the foundation for the next part, where we will delve deeper into understanding emotional triggers and the impact of self-awareness on personal growth and relationships. It's important to practice the of recognizing and naming emotions, as this is a fundamental skill in emotional intelligence.

Course 4

Emotional Self-Awareness Part 2

Emotional Triggers, Personal Growth, and Relationships

Learning Objectives for Course 4

1. Learn what emotional triggers are and how they impact our emotional state.

2. Gain strategies for identifying personal emotional triggers.

3. Understand the significance of emotional self-awareness in personal growth and relationships.

Course 4, Section 1

What Are Emotional Triggers?

Emotional Triggers: Unraveling the Links to Our Past

Definition of Emotional Triggers: Emotional triggers are specific events, scenarios, interactions, words, sights, or sensations that elicit strong, often automatic emotional reactions within an individual. These reactions can range from happiness and contentment to anger, sadness, fear, or anxiety. Essentially, when a person encounters a trigger, it's as if a switch has been flipped, prompting an immediate emotional response, often before the person has a chance to process or filter it through logical thinking.

The Origins of Emotional Triggers: To truly grasp the concept of emotional triggers, one must delve into their origins. Emotional triggers often have deep roots that stretch back to our past experiences, especially those from our formative years. Here are some ways in which they are intricately linked:

1. **Childhood Experiences**: Early experiences, particularly during childhood, play a pivotal role in shaping our emotional blueprint. A child who was constantly criticized might grow into an adult who feels defensive or insecure when receiving feedback. Another who was frequently left alone or felt abandoned might develop abandonment issues, feeling easily slighted or anxious in relationships.

2. **Past Traumas**: Traumatic events, whether experienced in childhood or adulthood, can lead to powerful emotional triggers. Someone who experienced a dog bite as a child might feel intense fear when seeing or hearing a dog, even decades later. Likewise, survivors of accidents or violent incidents might have strong reactions to sounds, places, or circumstances reminiscent of their trauma.

3. **Cultural and Societal Influences**: The societies and cultures we grow up in shape our values, beliefs, and notions of right and wrong. Actions or words that deviate from these norms can become triggers. For instance, in some cultures, direct eye contact might be seen as a challenge or disrespect, thus becoming a trigger for discomfort or anger.

4. **Relationship Histories**: Past relationships, whether familial, platonic, or romantic, also contribute to our set of triggers. For example, someone who has been betrayed in a past relationship might feel intense jealousy or suspicion when their current partner exhibits certain behaviors, even if they're innocent.

5. **Repressed Emotions**: Often, we might suppress or ignore certain emotions because they're too painful or because we've been taught that it's wrong to express them. Over time, these pent-up emotions seek an outlet. When faced with a situation that even remotely resembles the one, we've repressed, our reaction might be disproportionate to the current event because it's also releasing the tension of the past.

Understanding the Connection

Recognizing the connection between our triggers and our past experiences is a crucial step towards understanding ourselves better and cultivating emotional intelligence. When we begin to understand why certain things trigger us, we can approach these triggers with a sense of introspection rather than immediate reaction. This doesn't mean the triggers will disappear, but with awareness and practice, our response can shift from a knee-jerk reaction to a more measured, understanding, and intentional response.

Conclusion

In essence, emotional triggers are like portals to our past, providing us glimpses of unresolved issues, past traumas, or suppressed emotions. They offer us opportunities, albeit challenging ones, to confront, understand, and ultimately heal these aspects of ourselves. By doing so, we pave the way for more authentic, aware, and fulfilling interactions with ourselves and the world around us.

Course 4, Section 2

Identifying Your Emotional Triggers

Identifying Your Personal Emotional Triggers: A Guided Exercise

Introduction: Understanding our emotional triggers is essential for cultivating self-awareness. By pinpointing what sets off certain reactions, we can better prepare ourselves to handle such situations constructively. This exercise aims to help you reflect upon past experiences, identify the emotions they evoked, and pinpoint potential triggers.

Materials Needed:

1. A quiet, comfortable space
2. A notebook or journal
3. A pen or pencil

Instructions:

    1. **Find Your Calm**:

        a. Begin by sitting comfortably, closing your eyes, and taking a few deep breaths. This will help clear your mind and make you more receptive to introspection.

    2. **Recall Emotional Moments**:

        a. Think back to situations in the past month where you felt a strong emotional reaction. It could be a situation where you felt extremely happy, sad, angry, fearful, or any other intense emotion.

        b. Write a brief description of each situation.

3. **Describe Your Feelings**:

    a. For each situation, jot down the specific emotions you felt. Were you angry? Hurt? Jealous? Elated? The more specific you can be, the better.

    b. Beside each emotion, rate its intensity on a scale of 1 to 10.

4. **Identify the Trigger**:

    a. Reflect on what specifically within the situation triggered the emotion. Was it a particular word someone said? Was it a specific action or event? Or perhaps it was the environment you were in?

    b. Write down this specific trigger next to the situation.

5. **Seek Patterns**:

    a. Look over your list and see if there are any recurring triggers or themes. Do certain situations or types of comments consistently lead to certain emotions?

6. **Link to Past Experiences**:

    a. For any triggers that seem particularly strong or recurring, think about whether there's a past experience linked to it. Does the trigger remind you of something from your childhood, a past trauma, or a previous life event?

7. **Interactive Questions**:

    a. For each identified trigger, ask yourself the following questions:

    b. Have I felt this way before? When?

    c. What would I say is the root cause of this trigger? Can I trace it back to a particular event in my life?

    d. How does my body typically react when this trigger is present? (e.g., tensed muscles, increased heart rate)

e. What immediate thoughts come to mind when I encounter this trigger?

f. How might I want to react to this trigger in the future?

8. **Reflect and Conclude**:

    a. Take a moment to reflect on what you've discovered about yourself. Recognizing your triggers is a significant step toward emotional self-awareness. By identifying them, you can work on strategies to manage or even neutralize them in the future.

Tips:

1. Approach this exercise without judgment. It's not about labeling emotions or triggers as 'good' or 'bad', but about understanding yourself better.
2. It's okay if you can't identify the root cause of every trigger. Self-awareness is a journey, and insights may come over time.
3. Remember, everyone has triggers. The key lies in recognizing and managing them effectively.
4. Consider revisiting this exercise every few months to track your growth and changes in emotional responses.

By routinely practicing this introspective exercise, you can cultivate a deeper understanding of your emotional landscape, empowering you to navigate life with greater clarity and resilience.

Course 4, Section 3
The Impact of Emotional Triggers

The Impact of Emotional Triggers

Understanding Emotional Triggers: Emotional triggers are specific events, situations, or stimuli that evoke strong emotional reactions in individuals. These reactions are often linked to past experiences, memories, or traumas. Because of this connection to the past, when a person encounters a trigger in the present, the emotional response might not always align with the current situation's demands. Instead, it harkens back to an older, perhaps unresolved, emotional context.

The Mismatch between Reaction and Situation: When a trigger is activated, the emotional reaction might seem disproportionately strong for the present situation. This is because the individual isn't just responding to the current event, but to a flood of past emotions and experiences linked to that trigger. These reactions can be deeply rooted and automatic, leading to behaviors that might not make logical sense in the present context.

Complications of Misaligned Reactions:

1. **Ineffective Problem-Solving**: Responding to a present situation with past emotions can hinder our ability to effectively address the current issue.

2. **Strained Relationships**: Overreactions or misaligned responses can confuse or hurt those around us, especially if they are unaware of our triggers.

3. **Personal Distress**: Encountering triggers without recognizing them can lead to heightened stress, anxiety, or emotional turmoil.

4. **Reinforcing Negative Patterns**: If we consistently react to triggers without awareness, we can unintentionally reinforce negative emotional patterns or behaviors.

Benefits of Recognizing Triggers:

By identifying and understanding our triggers, we can:

1. Navigate situations with greater emotional clarity.
2. Develop coping mechanisms to handle triggers when they arise.
3. Improve our interpersonal relationships by responding more appropriately to present circumstances.

Hypothetical Example:

Aaliyah and the Unexpected Criticism

Aaliyah always prided herself on being meticulous at work. One day, during a team meeting, her manager pointed out a minor error in her report in front of her colleagues. While the manager's tone was neutral and the mistake was indeed minor, Aaliyah felt a rush of shame, anger, and embarrassment. She snapped back defensively, causing an awkward silence in the room.

Upon reflection, Aaliyah recognized that her reaction was tied to her school days when she was once humiliated in class for a small mistake. That past event had created an emotional trigger around public criticism, however minor. In the present situation at the office, the criticism from her manager activated this trigger, causing her to react based on her past experience rather than the actual gravity of the current event.

By recognizing this, Aaliyah was able to understand the disconnect between her intense emotional response and the present situation. She worked on addressing this trigger, ensuring that in future situations, she could respond more proportionally and appropriately.

Conclusion

Understanding the impacts of emotional triggers and their roots can greatly assist individuals in making more informed and constructive choices in their reactions, fostering better personal and interpersonal well-being.

Course 4, Section 4

Emotional Self-Awareness and Personal Growth

Introduction

Emotional self-awareness isn't just about recognizing and naming our feelings; it's about understanding the roots of those feelings and how they impact our behaviors and decisions. By addressing our emotional triggers and being fully present in our reactions, we foster personal growth, enhancing our resilience and adaptability in the face of challenges.

Emotional Mastery: The Pathway to Growth

Emotional self-awareness allows us to:

1. **Navigate Life's Challenges**: When we understand what stirs our emotions, we can anticipate potential triggers and better navigate situations that previously might have thrown us off balance.

2. **Develop Resilience**: Recognizing our emotions and understanding their origins helps us recover from setbacks more quickly. Instead of being stuck in a negative emotional cycle, we can process, learn, and move forward.

3. **Adaptability**: Being aware of our emotions makes us more adaptable. We can adjust our behaviors and reactions based on our understanding of our feelings, ensuring that we're reacting to the present, not the past.

Inspirational Quote

"He who controls others may be powerful, but he who has mastered himself is mightier still." - Lao Tzu

Supplemental Material

The Story of Lola and Her Fear of Failure

Over Achiever

Lola had always been a top student and an overachiever. Yet, as she grew older and faced real-world challenges in her career, she often found herself paralyzed by a fear of failure. Every time she encountered a challenging task or a potential risk, her heart raced, and she felt an overwhelming urge to avoid the situation.

Through introspection and emotional self-awareness, Lola discovered that her fear stemmed from a childhood experience. As a young girl, she had once been reprimanded by a teacher in front of her classmates for giving a wrong answer. That embarrassment had grown into a deep-seated fear of making mistakes.

By recognizing this trigger, Lola could address her fear head-on. She began to challenge herself, taking on tasks she would have previously avoided. Each success, no matter how small, helped to erode her fear. Over time, Lola not only overcame her fear of failure but became more resilient and adaptable, able to face challenges head-on and learn from her mistakes.

Concluding Thought

Understanding our emotions and their triggers isn't about dwelling on the past; it's about paving the way for a brighter future. By confronting and understanding our feelings, we gain control over our reactions, empowering us to grow, adapt, and thrive in an ever-changing world.

> *"Your visions will become clear only when you can look into your own heart. Who looks outside, dreams, who looks inside, awakes." - Carl Jung*

By fostering emotional self-awareness, we not only learn about who we are but also pave the way for who we can become. We unlock a level of adaptability and resilience that can carry us through life's ups and downs, always pushing forward toward growth and self-improvement.

Course 4, Section 5
Emotional Self-Awareness in Relationships

Introduction

Relationships, whether familial, romantic, or platonic, are the very fabric of our lives. They bring joy, support, challenge, and growth. Yet, they are also intricate, demanding understanding, patience, and self-awareness. Emotional self-awareness, in this context, is the pillar upon which strong, healthy relationships are built.

1. **Nurturing Healthier Relationships**

Understanding Self, Understanding Others: When we're aware of our own emotions and the triggers behind them, we're less likely to project our insecurities, fears, or unresolved issues onto others. We recognize our feelings for what they are: personal reactions based on our individual experiences, rather than objective truths or shared realities.

Scenario: Mike used to get upset whenever his partner, Jenna, spent time with her friends without him. Upon reflecting on his emotions, he realized his feelings stemmed from past experiences of being excluded by friends. Recognizing this allowed him to communicate his feelings without blaming Jenna and to work on his own insecurities.

2. **Improved Communication**

Articulating Feelings: Emotional self-awareness empowers us to articulate our feelings more accurately. Instead of saying, "You're making me feel ignored," one might say, "I feel ignored when you look at your phone while I'm talking. It reminds me of past experiences."

Scenario: Sophia and Rahim had frequent disagreements about household responsibilities. Rather than accusing Rahim of not caring, Sophia, having reflected on her feelings, said, "When I end up doing more chores, I feel overwhelmed and underappreciated. It reminds me of how I felt in my previous relationship." This opened a productive dialogue between them.

3. Better Understanding of Others

Empathy Through Self-Awareness: Recognizing our emotions can lead to increased empathy for others. When we understand the complexities of our own feelings, we're more open to the idea that others also have multifaceted emotional lives.

Scenario: When Carlos's colleague, Amit, seemed distant at work, instead of assuming Amit had a problem with him, Carlos remembered times he felt similarly due to personal issues. This empathy prompted Carlos to ask Amit if everything was okay, learning that Amit was dealing with a family crisis.

Benefits in a Nutshell

> 1. **Decreased Conflict**: Understanding our emotions can help de-escalate potential conflicts, as reactions become based on clarity rather than misconceptions or projected issues.
>
> 2. **Deepened Connections**: Open and honest communication about one's feelings can deepen intimacy and trust in relationships.
>
> 3. **Improved Conflict Resolution**: With an understanding of underlying emotions, solutions can be tailored to address root causes, not just surface issues.

Concluding Thought

Relationships thrive in an environment of mutual understanding, respect, and open communication. Emotional self-awareness isn't just about understanding us; it's about creating a space where understanding can flourish. By acknowledging and communicating our emotions clearly, we pave the way for healthier, more fulfilling relationships. The journey of understanding oneself is also a journey of understanding others, leading to deeper, more enriching connections with those around us.

Supplementary Material: An Emotional Journey

Joy's Emotional Journey

Joy had always been a beacon of positivity at her workplace. Her colleagues often joked that her name fit her perfectly. However, beneath that joyful demeanor were layers of emotions Joy wasn't fully aware of. Recently, she found herself reacting sharply to comments and criticisms that she would typically brush off with grace.

It began with a casual remark from her boss, Mr. Carter. "Joy, the presentation was good, but it could've been better with more research," he said during a meeting. Instead of taking it as constructive feedback, Joy felt a sudden rush of anger and defensiveness.

That evening at home, her teenage son, Max, mentioned he'd forgotten to inform her about an upcoming school event. Instead of her usual understanding response, Joy snapped, "Why can't you ever remember things?"

She lay in bed that night, pondering her unusual reactions. She'd recently attended a workshop on emotional intelligence, where she'd learned about emotional triggers. Realizing she might be experiencing this firsthand, Joy decided to delve deeper.

Over the next week, Joy kept a journal, noting down instances where she felt strong emotional reactions. She observed patterns. Criticisms from authority figures, like Mr. Carter, triggered feelings of inadequacy, reminding her of her father's unending expectations. Forgetfulness from loved ones, like Max's oversight, tapped into her childhood memories of feeling overlooked in a large family.

Having identified these triggers, Joy took proactive steps. Before meetings, she'd take deep breaths, reminding herself that feedback was a path to growth. At home, she created an open dialogue with Max about their daily lives, ensuring they felt connected.

A challenging situation soon presented itself at work. A major project was handed to her team. Joy's ideas were frequently questioned by a new colleague, Damien. Instead of retreating or retaliating, Joy recognized her emotional trigger. She scheduled a one-on-one with Damien, explaining her perspective and listening to his. It turned out, Damien had valuable insights but struggled with communication. Together, they combined their strengths, resulting in a successful project.

Back home, Max started showing signs of academic struggles. Instead of reacting impulsively, Joy held her emotions in check. She engaged Max in conversation, learning about his struggles with a particular subject and his embarrassment in admitting it. She remembered her feelings of being overlooked and made sure Max felt heard and supported. Together, they worked out a plan, including tutoring sessions.

Joy's journey of self-awareness transformed her interactions. By recognizing and managing her emotional triggers, she not only improved her work dynamics but also deepened her bond with Max. Instead of being held hostage by her past, Joy learned to harness her emotions, steering them towards constructive outcomes, making her journey an inspiration to all around her.

This course focuses on deepening the understanding of emotional self-awareness, making it a crucial step in learners' journey towards greater emotional intelligence. As before, engagement and practical application should be encouraged to solidify the concepts.

Course 5
Emotional Self-Regulation Part 1
Understanding Emotional Triggers

Learning Objectives for Course 5

1. Deepen the understanding of emotional triggers and their impacts.

2. Learn practical techniques for responding to emotional triggers in a healthier way.

3. Explore the process of self-regulation and its role in managing emotional triggers.

Course 5, Section 1
Revisiting Emotional Triggers

Recap from Lesson 4: Understanding Emotional Triggers

In our last session, we delved deep into the concept of emotional triggers. Remember, these triggers are events, people, words, or experiences that provoke a strong emotional reaction within us. They often have roots in our past experiences, especially those that left significant emotional imprints on us. Some triggers are universal, like the pain of rejection, while others are deeply personal, linked to specific incidents in our past.

Joy's journey from the previous lesson exemplified how recognizing and understanding emotional triggers can lead to personal growth and healthier relationships. When she became reactive to feedback at work or forgetfulness at home, she realized these reactions were not about the immediate situations but were tied to unresolved feelings from her past.

Understanding Emotional Triggers: A Deeper Dive

An emotional trigger is not just an ordinary event that causes a fleeting emotional response. It is a powerful catalyst that can make us feel disproportionately upset, angry, sad, or anxious. Why? Because these triggers touch upon areas of past hurt, vulnerability, or unresolved conflict.

Imagine your mind as a vast library. Each book represents a memory. Now, think of emotional triggers as those old, dusty books in the corner that we seldom read, but contain stories that shaped our lives. When something or someone 'triggers' us, it's like a gust of wind flipping those book pages open, forcing us to revisit those tales, whether we're ready or not.

For many, these triggers are unconscious. We react without understanding why. It's as if our emotions have bypassed our logical mind, taking us straight into a state of distress. This is because our brain's primary goal is to protect us. When faced with a situation reminiscent of a past threat, our brain reacts instantly, putting us in a defensive mode before we even realize it.

But there's good news. Just as we can train our muscles, we can train our emotional responses. The first step, as we discovered with Joy, is recognition. By identifying and understanding our triggers, we gain the power to manage them. Instead of being slaves to our past, we can choose how we want to respond in the present.

Emotional triggers are not our enemies. They are signposts pointing us to areas of our psyche that need healing, understanding, or resolution. By acknowledging them, we not only grow as individuals but also enhance our relationships, because we respond from a place of awareness rather than reactivity.

In this lesson, as we progress further into emotional self-regulation, understanding these triggers will be our foundation. Because to regulate our emotions effectively, we first need to understand what sets them off.

Course 5, Section 2

The Impact of Emotional Triggers on Behavior

Introduction

An emotional trigger can lead us to react impulsively. When a trigger is pulled, so to speak, it sets off a chain reaction within our brain. Before our logical mind has had a chance to assess and respond to the situation, our emotional brain has already taken over, propelling us into a specific behavior. This immediate, instinctual reaction often serves a purpose – it's the brain's way of protecting us. But in the context of our modern lives, these reactions can sometimes be more harmful than helpful, leading us to act in ways we later regret.

Short Story: "The Forgotten Anniversary"

Sam and Emily had been married for five years. Their relationship, like any other, had its ups and downs, but they always found a way back to each other. Emily had grown up in a household where her parents often forgot important dates, leading her to feel unimportant and overlooked.

One day, Sam, caught up in an important project at work, forgot their wedding anniversary. Emily, coming home excitedly with a gift for him, found no reciprocation. Instantly, a deep well of emotions from her childhood surfaced. Without stopping to assess the situation, her triggered emotions led her to lash out at Sam, accusing him of not caring about her or their relationship. She brought up past arguments, making the situation more heated than it needed to be.

The next day, with clearer minds, Emily realized her intense reaction was not just about the forgotten anniversary but also tied to her childhood experiences. Sam, for his part, felt remorseful for forgetting, but was also hurt by the magnitude of Emily's reaction. They both regretted not handling the situation with more calmness and understanding.

Imagination Infographic

Chain Reaction of an Emotional Trigger

1. **Trigger Event**: Image of a calendar with a crossed-out anniversary date
   Caption: Sam forgets the anniversary.

2. **Past Memory or Experience**: Image of a young girl looking sad with forgotten birthday decorations in the background.
   Caption: Emily's childhood experiences of being overlooked.

3. **Immediate Emotional Response**: (Image of a thermometer with mercury rising to the top, indicating anger)
   Caption: Emily's instant anger and feeling of being unimportant.

4. **Impulsive Behavior**: (Image of broken dishes or a storm cloud to represent the argument)
   Caption: The heated argument that ensues.

5. **Regret & Realization**: (Image of a sun rising, indicating a new understanding or the dawn of a new day)
   Caption: Recognition of the disproportionate reaction and its link to the past.

Conclusion

Understanding the connection between emotional triggers and our behaviors allows us to recognize when we're about to act impulsively. By being aware, we can take a moment to breathe, reflect, and choose a more appropriate reaction, rather than letting past emotions dictate our actions. As we delve deeper into emotional self-regulation, this awareness becomes a vital tool in our emotional intelligence toolkit.

Course 5, Section 3
Introduction to Self-Regulation

Introduction to Self-Regulation

Definition of Self-Regulation

Self-regulation refers to the ability to manage and control our emotional responses, particularly in challenging situations or when faced with emotional triggers. It encompasses being aware of our emotions, understanding the reasons behind them, and choosing appropriate actions that align with our goals and values.

Importance of Self-Regulation in Managing Emotional Triggers:

1. **Reduced Impulsive Reactions:**

Without self-regulation, we are more likely to react impulsively to triggers. An impulsive reaction is usually based on our immediate feelings, which might not be the most appropriate or beneficial response.

Example: Rather than yelling at a colleague who made an unintentional mistake, self-regulation allows us to address the issue calmly and constructively.

2. **Improved Decision Making:**

Emotions play a significant role in our decision-making processes. When we're able to regulate our emotions, we make decisions that are more rational, thought-out, and aligned with our long-term goals.

Example: If someone receives negative feedback at work, rather than taking it personally and deciding to quit on the spot, they could take a moment to process, understand the feedback's context, and determine the best course of action.

3. **Enhanced Relationships**:

Emotional reactions can strain relationships. By being more in control of our emotions, we can communicate more effectively, understand others better, and reduce unnecessary conflicts.

Example: In a disagreement with a partner, instead of resorting to blame, self-regulation can help one listen, understand the partner's perspective, and come to a compromise.

4. **Stress Management**:

Recognizing and managing our triggers reduces the occurrence of stress and anxiety. Over time, with consistent self-regulation, we can decrease the number of events that elicit strong negative emotional responses.

Example: Someone with a fear of public speaking might feel immense stress before a presentation. By recognizing this trigger, they can employ relaxation techniques to manage their anxiety.

5. **Personal Growth and Resilience**:

Being in touch with and managing our emotions contributes to personal growth. It aids in building resilience, as we become better equipped to handle adversities and bounce back from challenges.

Example: After experiencing a personal setback, such as a project failure, self-regulation helps an individual analyze the situation, learn from it, and move forward with newfound insights.

6. **Enhanced Well-being and Mental Health**:

Chronic negative emotional reactions can impact our mental health. By practicing self-regulation, we foster a more positive emotional environment, contributing to overall well-being and reducing the risk of mental health issues.

Example: Instead of ruminating on a negative thought or event, self-regulation techniques can be used to shift focus to positive or constructive thoughts.

Conclusion

Self-regulation is akin to having an emotional thermostat. Just as a thermostat regulates temperature to keep a room comfortable, self-regulation helps us maintain emotional balance in our lives. By mastering self-regulation, we don't just avoid negative consequences; we actively create a life filled with better decisions, relationships, and overall well-being. In the context of emotional triggers, self-regulation is the bridge that allows us to move from mere reaction to thoughtful response.

Course 5, Section 4
Practical Techniques for Dealing with Triggers

1. **Deep Breathing**:

Description: Deep breathing is a simple but powerful technique that helps calm the mind and body. When we encounter a trigger, our body often goes into a "fight or flight" mode. Deep breathing helps in countering this reaction by activating the body's relaxation response.

How to Practice:

    1. Sit comfortably or lie down.

    2. Close your eyes and take a slow, deep breath through your nose.

    3. Hold your breath for a moment.

    4. Exhale slowly through your mouth.

    5. Repeat several times until you feel calmer.

One example is the 4:7:8 technique of a deep breathing pattern of the inhalation and exhalation process, with a timer (e.g., 4 seconds inhale, hold for 7 seconds, 8 seconds exhale). There are several other types of breathing patterns, and timing, for different situations, or desired outcomes, which can be easily researched.

2. **Mindfulness Meditation**:

Description: Mindfulness is about being present in the moment without judgment. By practicing mindfulness, we can observe our emotional responses without getting caught up in them, allowing for a more measured reaction to triggers.

How to Practice:

    1. Find a quiet place to sit comfortably.

    2. Close your eyes and focus on your breathing.

3. If your mind wanders or if you start to have emotional reactions, acknowledge them without judgment and return your focus to your breath.

3. Cognitive Reframing:

Description: Cognitive reframing is a mental technique that involves recognizing and challenging negative or irrational thoughts. By changing our perspective on a situation, we can alter our emotional response to it.

How to Practice:

1. Identify the negative thought.

2. Challenge its validity: Is it based on facts? Is it a worst-case scenario?

3. Replace it with a more balanced or positive thought.

4. Time-Outs:

Description: Taking a time-out means giving yourself a break from a triggering situation. It's an immediate way to prevent a rash reaction, allowing time for emotions to settle and for you to think clearly.

How to Practice:

1. Recognize when you're becoming overly emotional.

2. Excuse yourself from the situation, if possible.

3. Engage in a calming activity: it could be a short walk, listening to music, or just sitting quietly.

4. Return to the situation when you feel more composed.

Conclusion

Understanding and identifying emotional triggers is just the first step. Applying practical techniques like deep breathing, mindfulness, cognitive reframing, and taking time-outs can significantly help in managing and regulating our responses to these triggers. Remember, the goal is not to avoid emotions, but to navigate through them with self-awareness and control. These techniques, when practiced regularly, can assist in achieving that objective, leading to a more balanced and harmonious life.

Course 5, Section 5

The Road to Mastery

Practice to Master

Every skill, be it riding a bicycle, learning to play a musical instrument, or managing our emotions, requires time, patience, and consistent practice. The ability to effectively deal with emotional triggers is no different. Like any muscle in the body, our emotional self-regulation muscle grows stronger with practice and repetition.

Emotional responses, especially to deep-seated triggers, often have roots in years or even decades of experiences and conditioning. Therefore, it's unrealistic to expect instantaneous change. The journey towards mastery in dealing with emotional triggers will have its ups and downs. But with every challenge faced and every trigger managed, we become better equipped to handle future emotional turbulences.

A Story of Perseverance: Maya's Journey

Maya was known for her fiery temper. As a child, feeling unheard led her to shout louder and become angrier. As she grew up, this translated into severe reactions to any perceived criticism. Her immediate defensive reactions cost her friendships, strained family relations, and even led to issues at work.

One day, after a particularly heated argument with a close friend who then distanced herself, Maya decided she needed to change. She recognized that her triggers were rooted in her childhood, where she felt overshadowed and overlooked. Armed with this realization, Maya decided to embark on a journey to understand and manage her triggers.

She started with mindfulness practices, often catching herself mid-reaction and taking deep breaths to calm herself. Every evening, she would journal about instances where she felt triggered, trying to cognitively reframe her initial perceptions. There were days when she felt she regressed, reacting impulsively, but she persisted.

Months passed, and slowly, Maya began noticing changes. Instead of snapping at a coworker's feedback, she'd pause, breathe, and respond calmly. Instead of getting into an argument, she started communicating her feelings more openly. People around her began to notice the transformation too. Relationships improved, and her work environment became more harmonious.

Years later, Maya became a mentor for many in her workplace, often sharing her journey and the tools she employed. She was living proof that with self-awareness, patience, and persistent effort, one could master the art of dealing with emotional triggers.

Conclusion

Mastery is a journey, not a destination. Just as Maya transformed her life through consistent effort, so can anyone be willing to put in the work? The key is persistence, patience, and the belief that change is possible. Every trigger managed, every emotion understood, brings us one step closer to our best self. Celebrate the small victories, learn from the setbacks, and remember, every day is another opportunity to grow.

Supplementary Material: Unexpected Reminders as Triggers

Navigating the Unexpected Storm

The sun painted golden streaks across the sky as Javier strolled to his favorite café after a long day at work. He was looking forward to catching up with an old friend, Derek, whom he hadn't seen in years. But the sun outside did little to hint at the storm Javier would soon face.

As he settled into a seat near the window, Derek walked in. They exchanged warm greetings, recounting memories from the past and sharing updates on their lives. But as the conversation flowed, Derek brought up a past event Javier had long buried.

"Remember that time in college when you totally blew that group project? Man, we all had to scramble to pick up the slack. It was chaos!" Derek chuckled, seemingly reminiscing about a humorous memory.

Javier felt a familiar heat rise in his chest. That incident was one of his most regrettable mistakes, a time when he'd taken on too much, and his pride prevented him from asking for help. The embarrassment, the guilt, and the feeling of letting his team down had haunted him for years. It was an emotional trigger he hadn't faced in a long time.

Old Javier might have snapped, perhaps defended himself angrily or shut down entirely. But recent self-awareness lessons had taught him the importance of recognizing and regulating such triggers. He took a deep, conscious breath, using the technique he'd practiced countless times before. As he exhaled, he allowed the initial rush of emotions to flow without judgment. Mindfulness had taught him to create a small space between stimulus and reaction, and he needed that space now.

"I know it must've been hard for all of you," Javier began, his voice calm and steady, "I regret not communicating my struggles during that project. It taught me a valuable lesson in teamwork and humility."

Derek, perhaps sensing the gravity of his words, softened his expression. "I didn't mean to bring it up as a jab, Jav. It's just one of those college memories that stuck, you know?"

Javier smiled gently, using cognitive reframing to shift his perspective. He recognized that while the memory was painful for him, for Derek, it was just a quirky college story with no malice attached. "It's okay, Derek. We've all grown since then. I just hope I've become a better team player."

The conversation shifted to lighter topics, and the evening wore on pleasantly. But for Javier, the real victory lay in navigating his emotional storm. Not only had he prevented an outburst, but he also managed to communicate his feelings without creating conflict.

As he walked home that night, the city lights shimmered in reflection on the puddles from a brief rain shower. Like the city, Javier too had seen a storm and its subsequent calm. He felt a deep sense of pride. The techniques he'd learned and practiced weren't just theoretical—they were tools that empowered him to sail smoothly even when unexpected storms hit.

Note: This story integrates the core elements of lesson 5, emphasizing emotional triggers, self-recognition, and the use of self-regulation techniques to navigate challenging situations.

Parting Thought

The focus of this course is to empower learners with practical techniques to manage their emotional triggers. As with all courses, engagement through practical exercises and self-reflection will be crucial to consolidate the learning experience.

Course 6
Emotional Self-Regulation Part 2
Self-Soothing and Calming Techniques

Learning Objectives for Course 6

1. Understand the concepts of self-soothing and calming techniques and their importance in emotional self-regulation.

2. Learn a range of practical techniques for calming and soothing oneself when faced with strong or negative emotions.

3. Apply these techniques in practice scenarios and daily life.

Course 6, Section 1

What are Self-Soothing and Calming Techniques?

Definition of Self-Soothing and Calming Techniques:

Self-soothing and calming techniques are strategies and tools that individuals use to regulate intense emotional states or physiological arousal. They are designed to bring an individual from a heightened state of distress to a state of relaxation or equilibrium. These techniques can be especially valuable when facing situations that are emotionally overwhelming, triggering, or stressful. They are the foundations for emotional stability.

Understanding the Need for Self-Soothing:

Throughout our lives, we are bound to encounter scenarios that challenge our emotional balance. These could range from minor inconveniences, like a flat tire, to major life events, such as the loss of a loved one. Regardless of the magnitude, our emotional responses to these events can sometimes be overwhelming. Enter self-soothing and calming techniques: the emotional equivalent to a first-aid kit. These techniques are immediate interventions we can apply to manage and mitigate distressing feelings and help maintain our emotional equilibrium.

Components of Self-Soothing and Calming Techniques:

1. **Physical Techniques**: These primarily involve bodily actions to counteract the physiological symptoms of distress. Examples include deep breathing exercises, progressive muscle relaxation, or even a calming walk.

2. **Mental Techniques**: These strategies revolve around harnessing the power of the mind to redirect or reframe our thoughts. Techniques might involve meditation, visualization, or cognitive reframing.

3. **Sensory Techniques**: Engaging the senses can often have a profound calming effect. This could be achieved by listening to soothing music, lighting a scented candle, or taking a warm bath.

4. **Distraction Techniques**: Sometimes, the best way to calm oneself is to divert attention from the stressor. Activities such as reading a book, drawing, or journaling can serve as effective distractions.

Role of Self-Soothing and Calming Techniques in Emotional Self-Regulation:

1.**Immediate Relief**: Much like how a painkiller offers instant relief from a headache, self-soothing techniques can provide immediate respite from intense emotions. They act as a buffer, preventing impulsive reactions.

2.**Promoting Emotional Awareness**: As individuals practice these techniques, they become more attuned to their emotional states. Recognizing when one is getting overwhelmed is the first step in applying a suitable calming technique.

3.**Encouraging Healthy Coping**: Relying on self-soothing and calming techniques promotes healthier coping mechanisms. It prevents individuals from resorting to detrimental coping strategies like substance abuse or emotional outbursts.

4.**Building Resilience**: Over time, the regular practice of these techniques can bolster emotional resilience. This means that when faced with future stressors, the individual is better equipped to handle them without becoming overly distressed.

5.**Improving Overall Well-being**: Beyond just managing distress, these techniques can enhance one's overall emotional well-being. Regularly practiced techniques, especially mindfulness and meditation, have been linked to increased contentment and reduced levels of chronic stress.

Conclusion

In conclusion, self-soothing and calming techniques are essential tools in the toolkit of emotional self-regulation. They offer a way to navigate the inevitable ups and downs of life with grace, resilience, and composure. By mastering these techniques, individuals can ensure that they respond to life's challenges in a manner that is constructive and balanced, rather than reactive and chaotic.

Course 6, Section 2

Why are these Techniques Important?

Benefits in Managing Emotional Triggers:

1. **Immediate Emotional Regulation**: Self-soothing techniques provide instant relief by decreasing the intensity of strong emotional reactions. By grounding oneself in the moment, one can avoid reacting impulsively.

2. **Prevents Overshadowing of Rational Thought**: Intense emotions can cloud judgment. By calming down, one can think more clearly and respond to situations in a more rational and measured manner.

3. **Reinforces Positive Coping**: Over time, regularly turning to these techniques when faced with triggers reinforces healthier coping mechanisms and reduces the reliance on potentially harmful strategies.

Benefits in Reducing Stress:

1. **Physiological Benefits**: Techniques like deep breathing can reduce the heart rate, lower cortisol (stress hormone) levels, and relax tense muscles. This not only feels better but also benefits overall health.

2. **Break from Continuous Stress**: In our fast-paced world, continuous stress can become the norm. Regularly practicing calming techniques can provide necessary breaks, reducing the risk of chronic stress.

3. **Improved Sleep**: Reduced stress levels, especially before bedtime, can lead to better sleep, which in turn has numerous health benefits.

Benefits in Promoting Overall Mental Well-being:

1. **Increased Mindfulness**: Techniques like meditation enhance mindfulness, which has been linked to greater life satisfaction and reduced symptoms of depression and anxiety.

2. Boosted Self-esteem: Successfully managing one's emotions can boost confidence and self-worth. Over time, one can develop a stronger belief in one's ability to handle life's challenges.

3. Enhanced Emotional Intelligence: Understanding and managing one's own emotions is a key component of emotional intelligence. This not only benefits personal well-being but also interpersonal relationships.

4. Builds Resilience: Repeated use and mastery of these techniques arm individuals with the skills to face future challenges, making them more resilient in the face of adversity.

Imagination Infographic

Benefits of Self-Soothing & Calming Techniques

Design: A tri-fold design, each section focusing on one of the three main benefit areas (managing triggers, reducing stress, and promoting well-being).

1. **Managing Triggers**:

    Icon of a brain with lightning (to represent triggers) being shielded by an umbrella (self-soothing techniques).

    Key Points from above listed below.

2. **Reducing Stress**:

    Icon of a stress ball being squeezed with a calm face on one side and a tense face on the opposite side.

    Key Points from above listed below.

3. **Promoting Well-being**:

    Icon of a person meditating, radiating a glow, with positive symbols (like a heart, a smiling face, and a peace sign) floating around.

Conclusion

In essence, self-soothing and calming techniques are more than just immediate fixes for intense emotions. They are vital tools that promote long-term mental health, resilience, and a more balanced approach to life's challenges. Whether faced with immediate triggers, enduring stress, or simply aiming for greater mental well-being, these techniques play a pivotal role in shaping a healthier emotional landscape.

Course 6, Section 3

Techniques for Self-Soothing and Calming

Techniques for Self-Soothing and Calming

1. Deep Breathing

Deep breathing involves taking slow, deep, and deliberate breaths. It increases the supply of oxygen to the brain, triggering a relaxation response throughout the body.

Imagination Diagram: Image of a person in a relaxed posture with arrows indicating inhalation and exhalation, accompanied by count numbers to show breathing rhythm (e.g., inhale for a count of 4, hold for 7, exhale for 8).

Imagination Infographic: Sequence showing:

- "Sit or lie down comfortably."
- "Close your eyes and focus on your breath."
- "Inhale deeply and slowly for a count of 4."
- "Hold for a count of 7."
- "Exhale slowly for a count of 8."
- "Repeat for several minutes."

2. Progressive Muscle Relaxation (PMR)

PMR involves tensing and then relaxing each muscle group in the body sequentially. It helps in releasing tension and promoting relaxation.

Imagination Diagram: Image of a body with highlighted sections indicating different muscle groups.

Imagination Infographic: Sequence showing:

- "Begin at your feet and work your way up."
- "Tense each muscle group for 5-10 seconds."
- "Release the tension and relax for 20-30 seconds."
- "Move on to the next muscle group."

3. Mindfulness Meditation

Mindfulness is the practice of focusing on the present moment, accepting it without judgment. It can reduce stress, increase self-awareness, and improve concentration.

Imagination Diagram: Image of a person in a meditative posture with thought bubbles depicting various senses (smell, touch, sound, etc.)

Imagination Infographic: Steps for a basic mindfulness exercise:

- "Find a quiet place."
- "Sit or lie down comfortably."
- "Close your eyes and focus on your breathing."
- "Notice sensations, thoughts, and sounds without judgment."
- "If your mind wanders, gently bring it back to your breath."

4. Visualization

Visualization is a relaxation technique where you mentally visit a peaceful or happy place. It provides a mental escape and induces a calm state.

Imagination Diagram: Image of a person with closed eyes, and a thought bubble showing a serene landscape, like a beach or mountain.

Imagination Infographic: Steps to visualize:

- "Close your eyes."
- "Imagine a place where you feel most relaxed."
- "Visualize every detail – sights, sounds, and sensations."
- "Deeply immerse yourself in this place for several minutes."

5. Grounding Techniques

Grounding techniques are strategies to help reconnect with the present moment. They're particularly useful during overwhelming emotional experiences or flashbacks.

Imagination Diagram: Image of two hands touching different textures (like soft, rough, cold, and warm) to showcase sensory grounding.

Imagination Infographic: "The 5-4-3-2-1 Grounding Technique":

- "5 things you can see."
- "4 things you can touch."
- "3 things you can hear."
- "2 things you can smell."
- "1 thing you can taste."

Conclusion

Incorporating these techniques into daily routines or using them during times of stress can make a significant difference in overall emotional well-being. Visual aids are particularly useful as they provide a clear and concise way to understand and adopt each technique.

Course 6, Section 4

Applying the Techniques in Practice Scenarios

Scenario 1: Minor Annoyance Situation: You're at home trying to focus on a task, but there's a constant dripping sound from a leaky faucet in the next room.

Technique to Apply: Mindfulness Meditation

- Sit down and close your eyes.
- Instead of feeling irritated by the dripping sound, use it as a focal point for your meditation.
- Pay attention to the rhythm and sound of each drop. Let other thoughts come and go without dwelling on them.
- By turning your focus onto the drip, you can transform an annoyance into a point of concentration.

Scenario 2: Moderate Stressor Situation: You're in traffic, running late for an important meeting.

Technique to Apply: Deep Breathing

- Turn off the radio and place your hands on the steering wheel.
- Take a deep breath in for a count of four, hold for four, and exhale for a count of four.
- As you breathe, remind yourself that you can't control the traffic, only your reaction to it.

Scenario 3: Daily Routine Stress Situation: You've had a long day of back-to-back online meetings, and your eyes and mind are exhausted.

Technique to Apply: Visualization

- Find a quiet corner or even just recline in your chair.
- Close your eyes and imagine you are in a calm, serene place – maybe a beach with gentle waves or a quiet forest with birds chirping.

- Imagine the sensations associated with that place. The warmth of the sun, the softness of the sand, or the cool breeze.
- Let this visualization rejuvenate your senses before you move on to the next task.

Scenario 4: Unexpected Challenge Situation: You receive an email from a colleague criticizing a project you worked hard on, and you can feel your heart racing and cheeks reddening.

Technique to Apply: Progressive Muscle Relaxation (PMR)

- Sit comfortably in your chair.
- Starting from your toes, tense each muscle group for 5-10 seconds and then release.
- Work your way up your body, from your legs to your abdomen, hands, arms, shoulders, and finally your face.
- As you work through each muscle group, you'll likely find the initial tension from the email dissipating.

Scenario 5: Major Stressor Situation: A loved one calls to tell you they've had an accident. They're okay, but you're left shaking and overwhelmed.

Technique to Apply: Grounding Techniques

- Use the 5-4-3-2-1 technique to bring yourself back to the present:
- Identify 5 things you can see around you.
- Touch 4 different textures (your hair, a desk, a cold windowpane, fabric of your clothes).
- Listen for 3 distinct sounds.
- Identify 2 different scents.
- Taste something (like sipping water or taking a deep breath).
- Grounding will help center you, making it easier to process the information and decide on next steps.

By working through these scenarios, students can practice and hone their skills in using self-soothing and calming techniques. Each scenario provides an opportunity to not only understand the technique but to experience its benefits in real-time situations.

Course 6, Section 5

Techniques in Daily Life

Integrating Self-Soothing and Calming Techniques into Daily Life

Introduction:

Integrating self-soothing and calming techniques into our daily lives is not just about handling crises or significant moments of stress. It's about weaving these techniques seamlessly into our routines, allowing us to maintain a sense of calm, enhance emotional resilience, and be better equipped to deal with the unexpected challenges of daily life.

1. Start the Day with Mindfulness Meditation:

Rather than jumping out of bed and rushing into the day, dedicate the first 10 minutes of your morning to a quiet mindful session. Focus on your breathing, the sensations of your body, and the sounds around you. This sets a calm tone for the rest of the day.

Image: A person sitting on their bed or on a yoga mat in morning sunlight, eyes closed, in a meditative pose.

2. Use Commute or Transition Times for Deep Breathing:

Whether you're driving, walking, or using public transport, utilize these moments as opportunities for deep breathing exercises. It helps to center you and makes these often 'wasted' periods more productive.

Video Clip: A person in a car, at a stoplight, taking a few deep breaths or someone in a train/bus, headphones in, eyes closed, focusing on their breath.

3. Introduce Progressive Muscle Relaxation (PMR) Breaks:

Especially if you have a desk job, integrate PMR into your breaks. Tense and relax muscle groups to release the physical tension that accumulates from prolonged sitting.

Image: Illustration of a person at a desk, with labels indicating various muscle groups to focus on, from feet to head.

4. Visualization during Lunch or Coffee Breaks:

Midday breaks can be more than just about food or coffee. Take a few minutes to close your eyes and visualize a peaceful scene. It's a mental vacation and can make a huge difference in how you approach the second half of your day.

Video Clip: A person at a park bench or cafeteria, eyes closed, serene expression, as the hustle and bustle continue around them.

5. Grounding Techniques for Moments of Overwhelm:

When facing a moment of extreme stress or overwhelm, use grounding techniques to anchor yourself back to the present. Keeping a small textured object, like a stone or fabric swatch, in your pocket can be a tactile way to ground yourself.

Image: Hand holding a smooth stone, with the caption: "Your grounding anchor."

6. End the Day with a Reflection:

Before sleeping, spend a few minutes reflecting on the day. Recognize moments when you felt agitated and think about how these techniques could have helped or appreciate instances when you effectively used them.

Video Clip: Person in dimly lit room, perhaps writing in a journal or simply contemplating, with soft, calming background music.

Conclusion

By consciously incorporating these techniques into our daily routines, we create a toolkit that's always accessible. This proactive approach means we're not just reacting to stress but actively managing and often preventing it.

Supplementary Material: Calming after an Emotional Trigger

Audio Narrative: Jun's Dual Approach to Stress Management

Background Music: Soft, calming instrumental.

Narrator: Jun's day had taken an unexpected turn. After a prolonged meeting with an unsatisfied client, he could feel the tension creeping in. His heart raced, and a heavy weight seemed to press on his chest. But Jun knew he had the tools to handle this. Let's delve into Jun's dual approach to self-soothing in this situation.

Guided Meditation Approach

Background Sound: Gentle waves crashing.

Narrator: Jun finds a quiet corner in a nearby park. Sitting on a bench, he closes his eyes, ready to transport himself away from the turmoil of the day.

Jun (to himself): "I'll start with a guided meditation. Let the surroundings fade and focus inward."

Jun's Inner Voice (calm, soothing tone): "Imagine you are on a serene beach. The sun is setting, casting a warm orange and pink hue over the sky."

Background Sound: Seagulls and waves

Jun's Inner Voice: "Feel the soft, cool sand under your feet. Each grain feels like a tiny massage, grounding you to this tranquil place. The rhythmic sound of the waves crashing is a reminder that life has its ebbs and flows."

Pause for breathing.

Jun's Inner Voice: "Breathe in the salty, fresh air, and exhale out all the tensions and worries. With each breath, you're becoming more relaxed, more present. The vast ocean before you symbolize endless possibilities and the vastness of life beyond this single stressful moment."

Background Sound: Waves become louder, more pronounced.

Jun's Inner Voice: "Imagine releasing all your stress and anxiety into the ocean. With each wave that comes to the shore, it takes away a bit of your tension, pulling it into its vast depths. You're left feeling lighter, clearer, and calmer."

Pause for breathing.

Jun's Inner Voice: "Slowly bring yourself back, holding onto the calmness of the beach. As you open your eyes, know that you can return to this place whenever you need."

Progressive Muscle Relaxation Approach

Background Sound: Gentle hum, indicating a quiet space.

Narrator: Later in the week, another stressful situation arises. This time, Jun decides to use Progressive Muscle Relaxation. Sitting comfortably in his chair, he begins.

Jun's Inner Voice: "Start by taking three deep breaths, inflating your lungs fully and exhaling slowly."

Pause for breathing.

Jun's Inner Voice: "Now, focus on your feet. Tighten the muscles in your toes. Hold for a count of five... and release. Feel the sensation as the tension melts away."

Narrator: Jun continues to guide himself upwards.

Jun's Inner Voice: "Now, tense the muscles in your calves. Feel the tightness... Hold for five seconds... and release. Let go of all the strain."

Pause for relaxation.

Jun's Inner Voice: "Move up to your thighs. Tense them as if you're trying to hold something between your knees. Feel the pressure... hold... and release."

Narrator: Jun can already feel the difference, but he continues.

Jun's Inner Voice: "Tighten your abdominal muscles, like bracing for a punch. Hold that tension... now, let it go, feeling the wave of relaxation."

Narrator: As Jun nears the top, he can sense his earlier stress dissipating.

Jun's Inner Voice: "Clench your fists, tightening the muscles in your arms and biceps. Hold it... and now release. Let the sensation of relaxation flow from your fingers to your shoulders."

Jun's Inner Voice: "Finally, scrunch your face, tightening all its muscles. Hold this for five seconds... and now release. Feel the calm wash over your entire body."

Narrator: Both techniques, though different in their approach, offered Jun an immediate refuge from stress. He had learned to be his own anchor, navigating through the stormy seas of life's challenges. And so can we all, with a little practice and presence of mind.

Background Music: Soft instrumental fades out.

Parting Thought

Engaging learners in practical exercises is crucial for this course, as the effectiveness of these techniques is highly experiential. It would be beneficial to encourage learners to keep a journal of their experiences as they experiment with these techniques in their daily lives.

Course 7
Emotional Self-Regulation Part 3
Cognitive Reappraisal and Handling Intense Emotions

Learning Objectives for Course 7

1. Understand the concept of cognitive reappraisal and its importance in emotional regulation.

2. Learn about cognitive distortions and how they affect our emotional responses.

3. Master techniques for cognitive reappraisal and handling intense emotions.

4. Apply these strategies in real-life scenarios and daily life.

Course 7, Section 1
Understanding Cognitive Reappraisal

Definition:

Cognitive reappraisal is a psychological technique and core component of emotional regulation. It involves changing the trajectory of emotional responses by reinterpreting the meaning of the emotional stimulus. In simpler terms, it's about changing our emotional reaction by rethinking or "reappraising" the situation that caused it.

The Process of Cognitive Reappraisal:

1. **Recognition**: The initial step is recognizing the emotional response and its cause. This involves being in touch with one's feelings and understanding what specific event or thought led to the emotional surge.

2. **Pause and Reflect**: Before reacting, one takes a moment to pause and reflect on the situation. This momentary step back allows a buffer between the stimulus (the cause of the emotion) and the response.

3. **Rethink**: Here, the individual tries to view the situation from a different perspective. This might involve questioning the accuracy of the initial interpretation or considering alternative viewpoints.

4. **Reframe**: After rethinking, the situation is reframed in a more positive or neutral light. This doesn't mean ignoring negative aspects, but rather focusing on other facets that might lead to a more balanced emotional response.

5. **Response**: With the reframed perspective, the emotional response might now be different — more balanced or even positive. This allows for a more thoughtful and measured action rather than an impulsive reaction.

Role of Cognitive Reappraisal in Emotional Self-Regulation:

1. **Balanced Reactions**: Cognitive reappraisal helps prevent extreme emotional reactions by offering a more nuanced understanding of situations. This prevents knee-jerk reactions that might not be in our best interest.

2. **Flexibility**: By practicing cognitive reappraisal, individuals develop the ability to adapt their emotional responses. This adaptability is crucial in our dynamic world where situations and stimuli constantly change.

3. **Stress Reduction**: By reframing stressors, individuals can often reduce the intensity of stress they feel, leading to better mental well-being.

4. **Improved Relationships**: When we react less impulsively and more thoughtfully, our interactions with others become more constructive. Misunderstandings can be reduced, and conflicts can be resolved more amicably.

5. **Growth and Learning**: Cognitive reappraisal is also a path to personal growth. By constantly reassessing our perspectives and feelings, we can learn more about ourselves, our biases, and our triggers.

Conclusion

In conclusion, cognitive reappraisal is a powerful tool in the emotional self-regulation toolkit. It's about challenging our immediate perceptions and reactions, offering us the chance to choose a more balanced and constructive emotional path. Like any skill, its effectiveness increases with practice, and over time, it can significantly enhance our emotional intelligence.

Course 7, Section 2

Cognitive Distortions and Emotional Responses

Definition:

Cognitive distortions are irrational or biased ways of thinking that can distort our perception of reality. These are patterns of thought that tend to magnify or minimize situations, negatively biasing our views and, as a result, our emotional reactions.

Examples of Common Cognitive Distortions:

1. **All-or-Nothing Thinking (Black and White Thinking)**: Viewing situations in absolutes, like "always," "never," or "every." E.g., "I always fail," or "I can never do it right."

2. **Overgeneralization**: Making broad interpretations from a single event. E.g., after a single rejection, thinking "Nobody likes me."

3. **Mental Filter**: Focusing exclusively on the most negative and upsetting elements of a situation, ignoring any positive aspects.

4. **Catastrophizing**: Anticipating the worst possible outcome from a situation. E.g., "I made a mistake at work; now I'm sure I'll be fired."

5. **Personalization**: Taking everything personally or blaming oneself for events beyond one's control. E.g., "The dinner party was a failure because I'm a bad host."

6. **Should Statements**: Having a strict list of what one should and shouldn't do and criticize oneself or others when those expectations aren't met.

7. **Emotional Reasoning**: Believing that what one feels is the absolute truth of a situation. E.g., "I feel stupid, so I must be stupid."

8. **Labeling**: Assigning labels to oneself or others based on limited information. E.g., "I'm a loser," or "He's so lazy."

Impact on Emotional Responses:

1. **Amplifies Negative Emotions**: By skewing perceptions towards the negative, cognitive distortions intensify feelings of sadness, anxiety, anger, and guilt.

2. **Reinforces Negative Patterns**: Because they validate and intensify negative feelings, cognitive distortions can become self-reinforcing, creating a vicious cycle.

3. **Inhibits Positive Emotion**: These distortions make it challenging to recognize, remember, or believe in positive experiences, leading to feelings of hopelessness or despair.

4. **Impedes Constructive Action**: Distorted thinking can hinder proactive behaviors or problem-solving as one gets mired in negativity.

Imagination Infographic:

Cognitive Distortions: Distorted Lenses of Perception

- [Image of a cracked lens] - Caption: "How we sometimes see the world through distorted views."
- Side 1: Distortions - List of the cognitive distortions with brief definitions and an icon for each. E.g., for "All-or-Nothing Thinking," an icon of a split black and white circle.
- Side 2: Impacts - List of impacts with related imagery. E.g., for "Amplifies Negative Emotions," an icon of an upward-pointing arrow with a sad face.

Conclusion

In summary, recognizing and challenging cognitive distortions is a key step in emotional regulation. By understanding these biases in our thinking, we can begin to see situations more clearly and react to them in more balanced and effective ways.

Course 7, Section 3
Techniques for Cognitive Reappraisal

Cognitive reappraisal is a key emotional regulation strategy that involves changing the trajectory of an emotional response by reinterpreting the meaning of the emotional stimulus. It's like "re-framing" your perspective on a situation to elicit a different emotional response.

1. **Identifying Cognitive Distortions**

Description: The first step is to recognize when you're caught in a distorted way of thinking. By naming the distortion, you can begin to dissect and challenge it.

Diagram: Flowchart starting with a thought bubble labeled "Negative Thought" leading to various labeled cognitive distortions with question marks, such as "Am I catastrophizing?"

Picture: Magnifying glass over a thought bubble, symbolizing the examination of one's thoughts.

2. **Evidence Checking**

Description: Assess the truth of your negative thoughts. Ask yourself: "What's the evidence for and against this thought?"

Diagram: Two-column table labeled "For" and "Against". On one side, there are tick marks, and on the other side, there are cross marks, representing evidence that supports or refutes the thought.

Picture: A balance scale, with evidence weighing down one side, illustrating the need to weigh evidence.

3. Perspective Shifting

Description: This involves asking how someone else would view the situation or considering how you might view the situation if you were an outside observer.

Diagram: A split image showing the same scene from two different angles or viewpoints.

Picture: A pair of shoes, symbolizing "putting oneself in another's shoes" to see their perspective.

4. Decatastrophizing

Description: Challenge the worst-case scenario by considering a) the probability of it happening, b) the best-case scenario, and c) the most likely scenario.

Diagram: A flowchart with a thought bubble labeled "Worst Case" branching out to three outcomes: "Likely", "Unlikely", and "Best Case".

Picture: A winding road leading to different destinations, symbolizing various possible outcomes.

5. Positive Reframing

Description: Focus on any potential positives or silver linings in a situation. Even in negative circumstances, there can be a lesson learned or growth opportunity.

Diagram: A picture frame, half showing a dark cloud and the other half showing a silver lining.

Picture: A plant growing out of cracked ground, representing growth in adversity.

6. Double Standard Technique

Description: Speak to yourself as you would speak to a dear friend in the same situation. Often, we're kinder to others than to ourselves.

Diagram: Two speech bubbles, one labeled "Self-talk" with a negative statement, the other labeled "Friend-talk" with a kinder version of the same statement.

Picture: A person looking in a mirror, seeing a friend's reflection, symbolizing self-compassion.

Conclusion

In summary, cognitive reappraisal is a vital skill in emotional regulation. By adjusting our perceptions, gathering evidence, and challenging distortions, we can better control our emotional responses and navigate life's challenges with more resilience and clarity.

Course 7, Section 4
Handling Intense Emotions

Intense emotions can be overwhelming. They can flood our minds, making it hard to think clearly, and might influence us to act impulsively. But, equipped with the right strategies, we can navigate through these emotional torrents with clarity and calmness.

1. **Recognizing the Emotion**: Before you can handle the emotion, you need to identify it. By naming the emotion, you take the first step in controlling it.

Picture: A face depicting an emotion with a label beneath it, e.g., "Anger", "Sadness", or "Joy".

2. **Deep Breathing**: Return to the calming techniques you've learned. Deep breathing can slow down a racing heart and provide oxygen to the brain, allowing clearer thought.

Picture: An individual taking a deep breath with arrows indicating the flow of breath.

3. **Grounding Techniques**: Bring yourself back to the present moment. The "5-4-3-2-1" technique is effective: Identify five things you can see, four you can touch, three you can hear, two you can smell, and one you can taste.

Picture: Hands touching various textures, with numbers descending from 5 to 1.

4. **Cognitive Reappraisal**: Use the strategies we discussed in the previous section. Challenge negative thought patterns, look for evidence, and shift your perspective.

Picture: Brain with two areas highlighted: one dark (representing the negative thought) and one illuminated (representing the reappraised thought).

Guided Audio Exercise 1: Grounding in the Moment

Begin with soft, calming music playing in the background.

"Close your eyes gently. Take a deep breath in... and out. Feel your feet on the ground. Notice the weight of your body on the chair or floor. You are here, at this moment.

Now, open your eyes and look around you. Name five things you can see. (Pause) Four things you can touch. Reach out and feel them. (Pause) Three things you can hear. Listen closely. (Pause) Two things you can smell. Inhale deeply. (Pause) And one thing you can taste, even if it's just the taste of the air or the lingering flavor of your last meal.

Breathe in... and out. You are here, in the present. Hold onto this feeling as you move forward."

Guided Audio Exercise 2: Challenging Negative Thoughts

Soft instrumental music in the background.

"Find a comfortable position. Breathe deeply... In... and out.

Think about a recent situation that caused a negative emotion. Bring that thought to the forefront of your mind. (Pause)

Now, let's challenge that thought. Is this a cognitive distortion? Are you catastrophizing or over-generalizing? (Pause)

What's the evidence for this thought? And against it? (Pause)

Imagine a dear friend came to you with this thought. What would you tell them? Offer yourself the same kindness. (Pause)

Now, try to reframe or reappraise the thought. Is there a more positive or neutral way to see it? (Pause)

Take a deep breath... and release. Every time you challenge a negative thought, you strengthen your emotional resilience.

Conclusion

Incorporating these techniques into your daily life not only helps in moments of intense emotion but also builds emotional resilience over time. Practice makes perfect. The more you engage with these techniques, the more adept you become at managing intense feelings.

Course 7, Section 5

Applying Cognitive Reappraisal and Emotional Handling Techniques in Practice Scenarios

Case Study Practice Scenarios

Case Study #1

1. **Delayed Promotion**: Sarah has been eagerly anticipating her promotion at work. When she learns that it's been postponed due to budget constraints, she feels devastated, thinking, "I'll never advance in this company."

Case Study: **"Delayed Promotion"**

Background:

Sarah, a dedicated employee of the 'Tec Solutions' company, had been awaiting her promotion for several months. She was given verbal affirmations from her superiors and even started preparing for the added responsibilities. However, when the day of announcement came, she was informed that due to unexpected budget constraints, her promotion, among others, had been postponed. Feeling a mixture of disappointment and insecurity, her initial thought was, "I'll never advance in this company."

Option 1: Identifying Cognitive Distortions

Sarah takes a moment to introspect and realizes she's catastrophizing the situation by believing she'll "never" advance in the company. Instead of letting this belief persist, she:

    1. Reflects on past successes and affirmations from her superiors.

    2. Reminds herself that budgetary issues are external factors and not reflective of her worth or abilities.

    3. Writes down her achievements and contributions to the company to reinforce her value.

Option 2: Evidence Checking

Rather than succumbing to negative emotions, Sarah decides to evaluate the evidence supporting her thoughts.

> 1. She recalls recent successful projects she headed.
>
> 2. She remembers the positive feedback from her boss and colleagues.
>
> 3. Recognizing the lack of substantial evidence supporting her negative thoughts, she concludes that her worth isn't diminished by a temporary delay.

Option 3: Perspective Shifting

Sarah seeks advice from a trusted senior colleague, Mr. Williams, who has been with the company for over a decade. He shares stories of similar setbacks he faced, explaining how they turned out to be beneficial in the long run, offering opportunities he hadn't anticipated.

Realizing that setbacks can sometimes lead to unforeseen opportunities, Sarah:

> 1. Begins to look at the situation as an opportunity for further growth and preparation.
>
> 2. Considers the possibility that the delay might offer her a chance to lead even bigger projects in the future.

Option 4: Applying Self-Soothing Techniques

Feeling the weight of her disappointment, Sarah decides to use some self-soothing techniques.

> 1. She spends ten minutes in a quiet space, practicing deep breathing exercises to calm her racing heart.
>
> 2. She visualizes a peaceful scene — a quiet beach during sunrise — to bring tranquility to her mind.
>
> 3. Sarah then practices a grounding technique, listing five things she can see, four she can touch, three she can hear, two she can smell, and one she can taste.

Option 5: Seeking Feedback for Growth

Instead of dwelling on the setback, Sarah schedules a meeting with her supervisor.

1. She discusses her performance, seeking feedback on areas she can improve.

2. Sarah expresses her disappointment constructively, making it clear she's still very committed to her role and growth within the company.

3. Her proactive approach earns her even more respect from her superiors, and she gets assurance that her growth in the company is valued.

Conclusion:

While setbacks can evoke strong negative emotions, Sarah's journey in this case study demonstrates that applying techniques of cognitive reappraisal and emotional handling can turn disappointments into opportunities for growth, self-awareness, and resilience. The way one responds to challenges often defines their trajectory more than the challenges themselves.

Case Study #2

2. **Friendship Woes**: Carlos feels hurt when he sees pictures of his friends hanging out without him on social media, thinking, "They probably don't like me anymore."

Case Study: "Friendship Woes"

Background:

Carlos, a passionate photographer and nature enthusiast, has a close-knit group of friends. After a busy week at work, he took some time to scroll through his social media and found pictures of his friends hanging out at a local cafe without him. He felt a pang of hurt and exclusion. The thought that immediately came to his mind was, "They probably don't like me anymore."

Option 1: Identifying Cognitive Distortions

Carlos recognizes that he's "mind reading" or assuming he knows what his friends are thinking without any concrete evidence.

1. He reminds himself of the countless times they've included him in their plans and the many shared memories they have.

2. He considers the possibility that there might have been a logical reason he was not invited, which doesn't necessarily relate to his worth in the group.

Option 2: Evidence Checking

Carlos decides to approach the situation rationally and checks for evidence supporting or refuting his thoughts.

1. He recalls the recent occasions when his friends' showed gestures of affection and camaraderie.

2. He remembers times when he himself couldn't join due to work and other commitments.

3. Recognizing a lack of substantial evidence for his immediate assumption, he realizes his worth in the group remains unchanged.

Option 3: Perspective Shifting

Carlos thinks back to times when he met up with just one or two friends from the group due to circumstantial reasons.

1. He realizes that just because everyone wasn't present, it didn't mean they didn't value the absent friends.

2. He starts considering that this hangout could have been impromptu or based on availability and not a deliberate exclusion.

Option 4: Applying Self-Soothing Techniques

Feeling the emotional sting, Carlos uses self-soothing techniques to regain his equilibrium.

1. He takes a few moments to engage in deep breathing, focusing on the rhythm of his breath.

2. He immerses himself in a visualization exercise, imagining himself in a serene forest, the sun's rays filtering through the trees, bringing warmth and clarity.

3. Using grounding techniques, he reconnects with the present, reminding himself of tangible truths around him.

Option 5: Open Communication

Instead of harboring feelings of hurt and resentment, Carlos decides to communicate his feelings.

1. He sends a friendly message to one of the friends present at the hangout, mentioning he saw the photos and felt a bit left out.

2. His friend quickly responds, explaining it was an unplanned gathering after a workshop they all happened to attend. They hadn't thought to invite others because of the spontaneity.

3. Feeling reassured, Carlos understands the importance of not jumping to conclusions and the value of open communication.

Conclusion:

Social media can sometimes inadvertently amplify feelings of exclusion and self-doubt. In Carlos's journey, the techniques of cognitive reappraisal and emotional handling not only alleviated his immediate feelings of hurt but also strengthened his bonds through open communication. Emotional intelligence equips individuals with the tools to navigate the often-complex world of interpersonal relationships with grace and understanding.

Case Study #3

3. **Project Setback**: Aman's project proposal is rejected by his supervisor. He immediately thinks, "I'm incompetent and unfit for this job."

Case Study: **"Project Setback"**

Background:

Aman is a hardworking project manager at a leading tech firm. He has always been proud of his innovative ideas. After weeks of burning the midnight oil, he finally presents his project proposal to his supervisor. However, the proposal is met with rejection. A sinking feeling engulfs Aman, and he immediately thinks, "I'm incompetent and unfit for this job."

Option 1: Identifying Cognitive Distortions

Aman realizes he's indulging in "catastrophic thinking," assuming the worst possible outcome from one setback.

>1. He recalls previous successful projects he's managed and the appreciation he received for them.

>2. He understands that one rejection doesn't define his entire career or abilities.

Option 2: Evidence Checking

To ensure he doesn't base his reactions solely on emotion, Aman weighs the evidence supporting or opposing his initial thought.

>1. He lists down all his achievements and positive feedback received over the years.

>2. He recalls instances where initial setbacks eventually led to greater outcomes once revised.

>3. Recognizing the numerous successes against one setback, he acknowledges that he's far from incompetent.

Option 3: Perspective Shifting

Aman takes a step back to consider alternative explanations for the rejection.

>1. He thinks about the possibility that the rejection might be due to budget constraints, changes in company direction, or external factors unrelated to his competence.

2. He reflects on the fact that constructive criticism can offer new avenues for improvement and growth.

Option 4: Applying Self-Soothing Techniques

Still feeling disappointed, Aman decides to use self-soothing techniques to calm himself.

1. He finds a quiet corner and engages in deep breathing, inhaling positivity and exhaling doubt.

2. He mentally travels to his 'happy place' — a calm beach during sunset, letting the soothing waves wash away his apprehensions.

3. Through grounding exercises, he reminds himself of his potential and focuses on tangible accomplishments in his professional journey.

Option 5: Seeking Feedback

Rather than dwelling on his feelings, Aman sees this as an opportunity to grow and improve.

1. He approaches his supervisor and asks for specific feedback on why the proposal was rejected.

2. His supervisor clarifies that while the idea was great, it needed more alignment with the company's current goals.

3. Grateful for the feedback, Aman understands the value of continuous learning and refinement in his profession.

Conclusion:

Facing rejection is a challenging ordeal in any profession. For Aman, the techniques of cognitive reappraisal and emotional handling not only prevented him from succumbing to self-doubt but also paved the way for personal growth and development. Such tools enable individuals to confront setbacks constructively, transforming potential pitfalls into opportunities for enrichment.

Interactive Role-Playing Practice Activities

Activity 1: Workplace Challenge

Scenario: You are a manager, and your colleague Alex approaches you, upset that their idea was not included in the final presentation. Alex says, "Every time I suggest something, it's ignored. Nobody values my input here."

Objective: Use cognitive reappraisal to address Alex's concerns.

Script:

> • Student (playing the manager): "I understand how you might feel that way based on this situation, Alex. Let's consider the past few months. Can you recall instances where your suggestions were taken on board?"
>
> • Role Player (playing Alex): "Well, yes. Last month my idea about the marketing strategy was used."
>
> • Student: "That's right. Sometimes, decisions are made based on a range of factors. It doesn't mean your input isn't valued. Let's discuss how we can incorporate your ideas in the future."

Activity 2: Friendship Misunderstanding

Scenario: You are having coffee with your friend Jamie. Jamie confides in you that they felt left out when they saw pictures of the group picnic you attended. Jamie says, "I saw everyone at the park on Instagram. I guess I'm not important enough to be invited."

Objective: Apply cognitive reappraisal to the situation.

Script:

> • **Student**: "Jamie, I'm really sorry you felt that way. The picnic was a last-minute plan made by Clara and Tom. I assumed they had informed everyone. Remember the movie night last week? That was your idea, and we all loved it!"
>
> • **Role Player (playing Jamie)**: "I know, but seeing those pictures made me feel isolated."

- **Student**: "It's completely valid to feel that way, but it wasn't intentional. Let's make sure in the future we keep everyone in the loop."

Activity 3: Negative Self-Perception at School

Scenario: You're in the school library, and your classmate Rahul approaches you, upset about getting a lower grade than expected. Rahul says, "I always mess up. I'm probably the dumbest person in class."

Objective: Encourage cognitive reappraisal.

Script:

- **Student**: "Rahul, one grade doesn't define your intelligence or capabilities. Remember when you aced the group project last semester? Or your brilliant presentation last month?"

- **Role Player (playing Rahul)**: "I do. But this grade makes me question myself."

- **Student**: "It's okay to feel disappointed. But instead of generalizing based on one outcome, let's focus on understanding what went wrong and how you can improve next time."

Conclusion:

These scenarios will help students apply the techniques of cognitive reappraisal and emotional handling in varied situations, strengthening their emotional intelligence and resilience.

Supplementary Material: Shifting Perspectives

Scripted Audio Narrative
Reframing Reality with Jamal

[Soft, ambient background music begins. A heartbeat sound effect slowly gets louder, then starts to fade, simulating an increasing heart rate that then begins to calm down.]

Narrator: Jamal, a dedicated high school teacher, stands before his class, handing back graded essays. As he distributes them, he notices several students whispering and looking at him with disappointment.

Jamal's Thought Voice: "They're not happy with their grades. They must think I'm a terrible teacher. Maybe I'm not cut out for this."

[Pause]

Narrator: But then, Jamal takes a deep breath, realizing he's spiraled into negative thinking.

Jamal's Thought Voice: "Wait a second... am I overgeneralizing based on a few students' reactions?"

[Pause as Jamal begins the process of cognitive reappraisal.]

Narrator: Jamal starts by identifying the cognitive distortion.

Jamal's Thought Voice: "Alright, I'm 'labeling and mislabeling' myself based on limited evidence. Not every student is unhappy. I need to think this through."

Narrator: Jamal then moves on to evidence checking.

Jamal's Thought Voice: "Remember last week when many students thanked me for clarifying complex topics? And what about the parent-teacher meeting where several parents praised my teaching methods?"

[Pause. We hear the sound of scribbling on paper – a student writing.]

Narrator: To get a clearer picture, Jamal decides on a perspective shift.

Jamal's Thought Voice: "Is it possible that their disappointment isn't about me? Maybe they're upset about their own performance or something else entirely."

[Sounds of school bell ringing. The chatter of students filling the room.]

Narrator: As the class ends, a student named Mia approaches Jamal.

Mia: "Mr. Jamal, I was surprised by my grade. I thought I did better."

Jamal: "I understand, Mia. Let's review your essay together and see where you can improve."

Mia: "Thanks, Mr. Jamal. It's not about your grading. I know I could've done better."

Narrator: This interaction validates Jamal's reappraisal.

Jamal's Thought Voice: "See? It's not about my teaching. It's about them wanting to excel. I'm here to guide them."

[Pause. Ambient background music continues softly.]

Narrator: At the end of the day, Jamal reflects on the incident.

Jamal's Thought Voice: "Today was a reminder. I need to avoid jumping to conclusions and practice cognitive reappraisal. Not every reaction is a reflection of my abilities."

Narrator: By understanding and applying cognitive reappraisal techniques, Jamal not only saved himself from unnecessary distress but also remained effective in his role as a teacher, guiding and helping students on their academic journey.

[The soft ambient music fades out, ending the narrative.]

Conclusion

This scripted audio narrative showcases the cognitive reappraisal process in action, offering learners a relatable scenario to grasp the techniques and their benefits.

Parting Thought

In addition to the structured course content, encourage learners to continue practicing these techniques in their daily lives. Keeping a journal to record experiences and reflections can help consolidate learning and promote self-awareness.

Course 8
Understanding Others' Emotions
Empathy

Learning Objectives for Course 8

1. Understand the concept of empathy & its role in emotional intelligence.

2. Learn to recognize and identify others' emotions effectively.

3. Master techniques for empathetic listening and response.

4. Apply these strategies in real-life interactions and relationships.

Course 8, Section 1
The Role of Empathy in Emotional Intelligence

Introduction:

Empathy is often considered the bridge of emotional understanding between individuals. At its core, empathy provides the ability to recognize, understand, and share the feelings of another, stepping into their "emotional shoes" so to speak. It's not just about feeling compassion, but genuinely understanding and connecting with another's emotional state.

Definition:

Empathy: The capacity to recognize, understand, and, in some cases, feel the emotions and experiences of another person. It's different from sympathy, where one might feel pity or concern for the sufferings of another but may not truly understand or share those feelings.

Empathy's Role in Emotional Intelligence (EI):

1. **Understanding Others**: At the heart of EI lies the ability to understand one's own emotions and those of others. Empathy enriches this understanding, allowing us not just to identify emotions in others, but to comprehend their origin and depth.

2. **Improved Interpersonal Relationships**: Empathy fosters deeper connections, promotes trust, and builds rapport. When someone feels understood, it can strengthen bonds and increase closeness.

3. **Effective Communication**: By understanding what others are feeling, empathetic individuals can adjust their communication style, ensuring their messages are received positively. This can lead to fewer conflicts and misunderstandings.

4. **Conflict Resolution**: Empathy allows us to see issues from another's perspective. This understanding can be vital in resolving disputes, facilitating a collaborative approach where all parties feel heard.

5. **Enhanced Teamwork**: In group settings, empathy can promote inclusivity and cohesion. Recognizing and valuing the emotional states of team members ensures that everyone feels valued and understood, leading to increased cooperation.

6. **Leadership**: Empathetic leaders are often more successful because they understand the needs, motivations, and emotions of those they lead. They can motivate, inspire, and address issues with a level of understanding that others may not possess.

Illustration: Imagine two friends, Alice and Bob. Alice is upset because she received criticism at work. Bob, showcasing sympathy, might say, "I'm sorry you had a bad day." While this is kind, it doesn't show deep understanding. However, if Bob showcases empathy, he might say, "I can imagine how that feedback made you feel undervalued and upset. Let's talk about it." The latter response doesn't just acknowledge the situation; it delves into Alice's emotions, offering genuine understanding and support.

Conclusion: Empathy is a cornerstone of emotional intelligence. It's more than just understanding that someone is feeling a certain way; it's about connecting with that emotion on a profound level. Through empathy, we can navigate interpersonal interactions more effectively, build stronger relationships, and foster a more compassionate and understanding world.

What's Next...

In the next section, we will explore different types of empathy and how they contribute to our interactions and understanding of others.

Course 8, Section 2
Recognizing Others' Emotions

Introduction:

Recognizing emotions in others is an essential first step in the process of empathy. Our ability to discern others' feelings is based on various signals that individuals emit, consciously or unconsciously. By becoming adept at reading these cues, we can better understand, communicate, and respond to the people around us.

Ways to Recognize Emotions in Others:

1. **Verbal Cues**:

    • **What They Say**: Sometimes, people explicitly express their feelings. For instance, "I'm frustrated" or "I'm elated."

    • **How They Say it**: Even when not directly stating emotions, the choice of words can hint at underlying feelings. Statements like "It's just one of those days" might imply a rough or tiresome day.

2. **Tone of Voice**:

    • **Pitch**: A higher pitch can indicate excitement, fear, or surprise, while a lower pitch might indicate sadness or fatigue.

    • **Volume**: A sudden increase in volume might hint at anger or frustration, while a softer voice might indicate sadness, fear, or insecurity.

    • **Pace**: Rapid speech can sometimes signify nervousness or excitement, while slow talk might suggest sadness, deep thought, or tiredness.

    • **Inflection**: The rise and fall in voice can convey various emotions; for example, an upward inflection can indicate a question or uncertainty.

3. Body Language:

> • **Facial Expressions**: The face is a window to our emotions. Raised eyebrows might show surprise, a frown could indicate sadness or discontent, and a smile usually signifies happiness or contentment. [Image of different facial expressions showing happiness, sadness, anger, surprise, and neutrality]
>
> • **Posture**: An upright, open posture often represents confidence or happiness, while slouched or closed-off posture can indicate sadness, defensiveness, or insecurity. [Image of a person standing confidently and another slouching]
>
> • **Gestures**: Hand movements, nods, and shakes can all provide insight into someone's emotional state. For instance, crossed arms might show defensiveness, while animated hand gestures could indicate excitement or passion! [Image of various hand gestures]
>
> • **Eye Contact**: Consistent eye contact might indicate interest and attentiveness, while avoidance might signify discomfort, guilt, or shyness.
>
> • **Physical Proximity**: How close a person stands or sits next to you can also hint at their comfort level and feelings toward you.

4. Contextual Clues:

> • Understanding the environment and context can greatly help in interpreting emotions. For instance, if someone is pacing back and forth in a hospital waiting room, they might be feeling anxious or worried.

Practice:

> • **Image Activity**: Show learners various images of people exhibiting different emotions and ask them to identify the emotion based on visual cues.
>
> • **Role Play**: Let two participants act out a scenario using certain emotional cues, while others try to decipher the underlying emotions.

Conclusion:

Understanding emotions in others isn't just about observing single cues but interpreting a combination of signals in their context. Recognizing these emotional signs enhances our capability to empathize, connect, and interact meaningfully with others. By improving this skill, we pave the way for deeper relationships, effective communication, and a more harmonious coexistence.

In the next section, we'll delve deeper into the importance of showing empathy and how it can positively influence our relationships and environments.

Course 8, Section 3

The Practice of Empathetic Listening

Introduction:

Empathetic listening goes beyond just hearing the words someone says, it's about truly understanding and feeling the emotions behind those words. By actively immersing ourselves in their perspective, we create a space where individuals feel seen, heard, and validated.

What is Empathetic Listening?

Empathetic listening is the act of being fully present and engaged when another person is sharing their feelings, thoughts, or concerns. It involves:

1. **Non-judgment**: Listening without forming opinions or making evaluations.

2. **Patience**: Allowing the speaker to communicate at their own pace without rushing or interrupting them.

3. **Validation**: Recognizing and acknowledging the person's feelings.

4. **Open body language**: Displaying interest and engagement through eye contact, nods, and facial expressions.

5. **Reflecting back**: Paraphrasing or summarizing what the speaker said to ensure understanding.

6. **Asking open-ended questions**: Encouraging deeper exploration of thoughts and feelings.

7. **Avoiding immediate solutions**: Rather than quickly providing solutions, empathetic listening prioritizes understanding the person's experience.

Supplemental Material: Empathetic Listening

The Weight of Silence

Anna had always been an extrovert, lively and energetic. However, recently, her coworkers noticed she'd been quieter, often lost in her thoughts. During lunch break, her friend Maya, concerned, decided to approach her.

"Hey, Anna," Maya began gently, "I've noticed you've been distant lately. Is everything okay?"

Anna hesitated, then sighed, "It's just... my mom's health isn't great. She's been diagnosed with a chronic illness, and it's been tough on my family."

Rather than jumping in with advice or sharing a similar experience, Maya remained silent for a moment, allowing Anna's words to linger. She maintained eye contact, her face reflecting genuine concern.

"I'm so sorry to hear that," Maya replied softly. "That sounds incredibly challenging. How are you holding up?"

Anna took a deep breath, "It's been hard. I'm trying to stay strong for my family, but some days it feels overwhelming."

Maya nodded, "It must be a heavy burden to bear. Remember, it's okay to lean on others during tough times. I'm here for you."

Anna's eyes welled up. "Thank you, Maya. Just talking about it feels like lifting a weight off my chest."

Maya smiled warmly, "Sometimes, all we need is someone willing to listen."

Conclusion

Empathetic listening is more than a technique—it's a way of connecting with another person on a deep emotional level. When we listen empathetically, we not only understand others better but also foster trust, strengthen relationships, and promote open communication. It's a practice that requires patience and intention but can lead to profound connections and support.

What's Next...

In the next section, we will explore the transformative effects of empathy on relationships and personal growth.

Course 8, Section 4
Responding with Empathy

Introduction:

Recognizing emotions in others is just one step in the process. How we respond to those emotions determines the strength and depth of our interpersonal connections. Empathetic responses can make someone feel heard, validated, and understood.

The Importance of Empathetic Responses:

Responding with empathy means engaging in the moment, prioritizing the other person's feelings, and conveying understanding. An empathetic response nurtures trust, enhances emotional bonds, and aids in conflict resolution.

Effective Responses:

    1. Validation: Recognize and acknowledge the other person's emotions, even if you don't fully understand them.

    2. Paraphrasing: Summarize what the person has said to show you're actively listening.

    3. Open-ended questions: Encourage deeper exploration and allow the speaker to share more.

    4. Offering comfort: A simple touch, nod, or gesture can go a long way in showing support.

    5. Avoiding solutions: Instead of providing immediate advice, prioritize understanding their experience.

    6. Expressing shared feelings: If you genuinely feel the same, it can be comforting for the other person to know they're not alone.

Role-Play Script

Scenario: Jake shares his stress about an upcoming job interview with his friend, Leah.

Jake: I've got that job interview tomorrow, and I'm honestly freaking out. I don't think I'm prepared enough.

Leah (Validating): It's completely understandable to feel that way, especially with something as big as a job interview.

Jake: Everyone says I should be fine, but I can't shake off this anxiety.

Leah (Paraphrasing): So, even though others are confident about it, you're still feeling really anxious?

Jake: Exactly. I just don't want to mess up.

Leah (Open-ended question): What's your biggest concern about the interview?

Jake: I guess... that I won't have the right answers.

Leah (Offering comfort): I've seen how hard you've prepared. But remember, interviews are a two-way street. They're getting to know you, but you're also getting to know them.

Jake: That's a good point. I hadn't really thought of it that way.

Leah (Expressing shared feelings): I remember feeling the same way before my first big interview. The anxiety is real, but I believe in you. And no matter what happens, it's a learning experience.

Empathetic Phrases and Statements:

    1. "I can see why you'd feel that way."

    2. "That sounds really tough; I'm here for you."

    3. "It's okay to feel this way."

    4. "Thank you for sharing this with me."

    5. "I'm genuinely sorry you're going through this."

6. "You're not alone in this."

7. "Take your time; I'm here to listen."

8. "How can I support you right now?"

Conclusion:

Empathy is an active process that requires genuine engagement. By mastering the art of empathetic responses, we can deepen our connections, offer support, and build stronger, more trusting relationships. The journey to understanding others starts with a single empathetic response. In the next section, we'll delve into the broader implications of empathy in a community setting.

Course 8, Section 5

Empathy in Action – Real-life Application

Introduction:

Putting empathy into practice is the true test of understanding. The theoretical knowledge is important, but actual application deepens comprehension and solidifies the skill. Below are several scenarios to practice and understand empathetic listening and response better.

Scenario 1: Difficult Break-up:

Anna recently broke up with her partner of three years. She tells her friend, "It feels like a part of me is missing. Everywhere I go, everything I do reminds me of him."

Interactive Component: How would you respond empathetically to Anna? Write down or share your response.

Scenario 2: Job Loss:

Michael confides in his colleague, saying, "I was laid off from my job yesterday. I have a family to feed, and I don't know what I'm going to do."

Interactive Component: How can you offer Michael an empathetic response? Share your thoughts.

Scenario 3: Academic Pressure:

Jenny is a high school senior. She expresses to her teacher, "Everyone expects me to be the top of the class, but the pressure is driving me crazy. I'm scared I'll disappoint everyone."

Interactive Component: Imagine you're the teacher. How would you comfort Jenny with an empathetic reply?

Scenario 4: Health Issues:

David, a young athlete, was recently diagnosed with a condition that might end his sports career. He vents, "Sports is my life. Without it, I feel lost and purposeless."

Interactive Component: How can you show understanding and support to David in this situation? Suggest an empathetic response.

Scenario 5: New City Blues:

Farah moved to a new city for her job. During a call with her old friend, she shares, "I feel so out of place here. Everyone has their groups, and I'm just the outsider."

Interactive Component: If you were Farah's friend, how would you reassure her using empathy?

Conclusion:

Everyday situations often require us to show understanding and empathy. By practicing and refining our responses in various contexts, we can be better prepared to offer comfort and support when it's needed the most. As a next step, students can discuss their responses, reflect on what makes a response genuinely empathetic, and learn from each other to improve their empathetic communication skills.

Possible Responses to each of the scenarios above

Scenario 1: Difficult Break-up

Anna: "It feels like a part of me is missing. Everywhere I go, everything I do reminds me of him."

Responses:

> 1. "I'm so sorry you're going through this, Anna. Breakups can be incredibly tough. Please know I'm here for you in any way you need."
>
> 2. "That sounds really hard, Anna. Remember it's okay to feel the way you do. Let's talk about it whenever you're ready."
>
> 3. "Anna, I can't imagine how tough it must be for you right now. But please know you don't have to go through this alone. I'm here for you."

Scenario 2: Job Loss

Michael: "I was laid off from my job yesterday. I have a family to feed, and I don't know what I'm going to do."

Responses:

> 1. "Michael, I can't fully understand how you must be feeling right now, but I'm genuinely sorry about the situation. Please let me know if there's any way, I can support you during this time."
>
> 2. "That's really tough, Michael. Remember, it's okay to feel overwhelmed. Let's discuss potential next steps, and maybe I can help in some way."
>
> 3. "I can't imagine how stressful this must be for you, Michael. I'm here to help in any way I can – whether it's looking for job leads or just listening."

Scenario 3: Academic Pressure

Jenny: "Everyone expects me to be the top of the class, but the pressure is driving me crazy. I'm scared I'll disappoint everyone."

Responses:

> 1. "Jenny, which sounds incredibly stressful. Remember that it's okay to seek help or take breaks when needed. You're not alone in this journey."
>
> 2. "It's tough when we feel like everyone's expectations are on our shoulders. But remember, Jenny, you're doing your best, and that's what truly matters."
>
> 3. "Jenny, I believe in you and your capabilities. But remember, it's okay to set boundaries for yourself. If you ever want to talk, I'm here."

Scenario 4: Health Issues

David: "Sports is my life. Without it, I feel lost and purposeless."

Responses:

> 1. "I can see how deeply this impacts you, David. It's okay to grieve this change in your life. Let's find ways together to help you find a new purpose."

2. "That's a tough pill to swallow, David. Remember that while sports are a huge part of you, it doesn't define your entire identity. I'm here to support you as you navigate this."

3. "It must be challenging to face this change, David. Let's talk about it, and maybe we can find ways to pivot and discover new passions."

Scenario 5: New City Blues

Farah: "I feel so out of place here. Everyone has their groups, and I'm just the outsider."

Responses:

1. "Adjusting to a new place can be really hard, Farah. Remember, it's okay to take time to find your footing. I'm here to chat whenever you need."

2. "Farah, I can imagine how isolating that might feel. But I believe with time you'll find your place and people who appreciate you for who you are."

3. "It's tough starting over in a new place, Farah. I'm always here for a chat or to help in any way I can. Remember, these feelings are valid, but they are also temporary."

Conclusion

These empathetic responses not only acknowledge the feelings of the individuals but also offer support, showing that they're not alone in their challenges.

Supplementary Material: "The Empathy Exercise"

The Empathy Exercise

Charice had always prided herself on being an excellent communicator. She was a team leader at a growing marketing firm and believed in clear, concise communication. However, when her teammate, Raj, began to lag in his performance, Charice found herself at a loss.

"Raj, we need those reports by tomorrow," she reminded him one day, a hint of frustration evident in her voice.

Raj looked up; his eyes shadowed with exhaustion. "I know, Charice. I'm doing my best."

Charice was about to retort with a sharp reminder about responsibility when she remembered a workshop she'd attended on emotional intelligence. She took a deep breath and shifted her approach.

"Raj, I've noticed that you've been off your game lately. Is everything okay?"

He hesitated, then sighed. "Honestly, Charice, it's been tough. My mother's been ill, and I'm the only one around to care for her. I've been struggling to balance work and her medical needs."

Charice felt a pang of regret for not noticing sooner. She realized that this was her moment to practice empathetic listening. She pulled up a chair next to Raj. "I'm so sorry to hear that. Tell me more."

As Raj opened up about his challenges at home and his feelings of being overwhelmed, Charice genuinely listened. She wasn't crafting responses or thinking of the next thing to say; she was entirely present for Raj.

After he'd finished, Charice took a moment to respond. "Thank you for sharing that with me, Raj. It sounds incredibly challenging. How can I, or the team, support you during this time?"

Raj seemed taken aback, likely expecting a different response. "Maybe I could adjust my work hours or get some temporary assistance with some tasks?"

Charice nodded. "Of course. Let's work on a plan together. And if you need any time off, just let me know. Your well-being, and your mother's, is crucial."

Raj smiled weakly. "Thank you, Charice. It means a lot."

From that day on, not only did Raj's performance improve with the adjustments, but the trust and rapport between him and Charice deepened. Charice also began integrating empathy exercises into her team's weekly meetings. It wasn't just about recognizing emotions; it was about validating them, understanding, and providing support.

The ripple effect of Charice's empathetic approach was profound. Team members felt seen and heard. They began to communicate more openly, not just about work but also about their personal challenges. Productivity increased, not because they worked longer hours, but because they worked in an environment where they felt valued and understood.

Months later, at the company's annual retreat, Raj stood up during an open mic session. "I want to thank Charice," he began, his voice steady. "During one of the hardest times of my life," she listened. She showed me empathy, and it made all the difference. It wasn't just about the job; it was about being human."

As applause filled the room, Charice realized that while data, strategies, and communication tools were essential, nothing could replace genuine empathy in building trust and connection. The empathy exercise wasn't just an exercise; it was a way of life.

Note: This story highlights the importance of recognizing emotions, listening with empathy, and responding with genuine understanding, showing learners the impact empathy can have in real-life situations.

Parting Thoughts

To reinforce learning, encourage learners to practice empathetic listening and responses in their daily conversations. Reflecting on these experiences and their outcomes can help consolidate their learning and improve their empathetic skills.

Course 9
Interpersonal Relationships Part 1
Communication and Conflict Management

Learning Objectives for Course 9

1. Understand the role of emotional intelligence in communication and conflict management.

2. Learn the techniques of effective communication and how to apply them in personal and professional relationships.

3. Understand the concept of conflict, its sources, and the role of emotions in conflict situations.

4. Learn the techniques of conflict management and resolution, focusing on emotional intelligence strategies.

Course 9, Section 1
The Role of Emotional Intelligence in Communication

Effective Communication Defined:

Effective communication is the act of conveying a message in such a way that it is clearly understood, well-received, and elicits the desired response or action from the recipient. This can involve spoken or written language, body language, tone, and active listening.

Role of Emotional Intelligence in Communication:

Emotional intelligence plays a pivotal role in making communication more effective. By being attuned to one's own emotions and those of others:

1. Self-awareness: One can better articulate feelings, needs, and concerns without letting emotions cloud the message.

2. Empathy: Understanding and validating others' emotions can build trust and rapport, making the exchange more open and genuine.

3. Self-regulation: This helps in managing impulsive reactions, ensuring the conversation remains constructive.

4. Social skills: With honed interpersonal abilities, one can navigate complex social situations, adjusting communication styles to suit different personalities or contexts.

Short Story: "The Forgotten Anniversary"

Maria sat at the dining table, disappointed that Tom had forgotten their anniversary. She'd expected a quiet dinner or at least a small token of appreciation, but he seemed oblivious.

She pondered confronting him, her initial thoughts tinged with anger: "How could you forget? Don't you care?" But her emotional intelligence kicked in. Instead of reacting impulsively, she considered her emotions and the potential reasons for his oversight.

Approaching him calmly, she said, "Tom, I feel a bit hurt that our anniversary slipped by without acknowledgment. Is everything okay?"

Tom blinked, realizing his mistake. "I'm so sorry, Maria. Work has been overwhelming, and I lost track of dates. I genuinely forgot, not because I don't care, but because I've been so consumed. I should have prioritized better."

Maria's approach, rooted in understanding her emotions and expressing them effectively, opened the door to a constructive conversation. Tom's immediate acknowledgment and apology showed the benefit of clear, emotion-aware communication.

Conclusion

In this story, Maria's emotional intelligence helped her convey her feelings without escalating into an argument. By recognizing and understanding her emotions, she crafted a message that allowed for open communication, thus enhancing the quality of their conversation.

Course 9, Section 2

Techniques of Effective Communication

Communication isn't just about speaking or conveying a message; it's also about ensuring that the message is understood and generates the desired response. Let's delve into some key techniques to enhance communication effectiveness.

1. **Active Listening**

    - **Definition**: Active listening means fully concentrating on, understanding, responding to, and remembering what the other person is saying.

    - **Application**: This involves not interrupting, giving feedback, refraining from formulating a reply while the other person is speaking, and clarifying points that seem ambiguous.

    - **Infographic**: A split image showing "Passive Listening" on one side (with a person distracted, looking at their watch) and "Active Listening" on the other (with a person making eye contact, nodding, and taking notes).

2. **Empathy in Communication**

    - **Definition**: Empathy is the capacity to understand or feel what another person is experiencing from within their frame of reference.

    - **Application**: It's crucial in communication as it helps to validate the other person's feelings, even if you don't necessarily agree with their perspective.

    - **Diagram**: A heart symbol with two speech bubbles emerging from it, one saying, "I hear you" and the other "I understand."

3. **Nonverbal Communication**

    - **Definition**: Nonverbal communication encompasses facial expressions, body language, tone of voice, and gestures that often speak louder than words.

    - **Application**: Being aware of your nonverbal cues and interpreting others' can significantly enhance understanding. For instance, crossed arms might indicate defensiveness, while maintaining eye contact can convey interest.

- **Infographic**: A body outline with arrows pointing to various body parts (eyes, arms, legs, posture) with short descriptors (e.g., "Eyes: Avoiding contact = Disinterest, Direct gaze = Attention").

4. **Assertive Communication**

    - **Definition**: Assertiveness is expressing one's views, needs, boundaries, and feelings in an open, honest, and respectful manner without violating the rights of others.

    - **Application**: It's the middle ground between aggression and passivity. For instance, instead of saying, "You never listen to me" (aggressive) or saying nothing (passive), you could say, "I feel unheard when we discuss this topic. Can we try a different approach?" (assertive).

    - **Diagram**: A continuum line labeled "Passive" on one end, "Aggressive" on the other, and "Assertive" in the middle. Each point can have a speech bubble illustrating the communication style.

Conclusion

Effective communication is multifaceted. By integrating these techniques into our interactions, we pave the way for clearer understanding, reduced conflicts, and more meaningful relationships. Always remember it's not just about the message you convey, but how it's received.

Course 9, Section 3

Understanding Conflict

Definition of Conflict:

Conflict refers to any situation where two or more parties perceive incompatible goals, values, or interests. It's an inevitable part of human relationships, arising from differences in needs, perceptions, or values.

Sources of Conflict:

    1. **Differing Needs or Expectations**: This could be in terms of resources, time, or priority.

    2. **Communication Barriers**: Misunderstandings often arise from not effectively communicating our needs or not understanding others.

    3. **Value Differences**: Our beliefs, traditions, and personal values can clash with those of others.

    4. **External Stressors**: External pressures like financial problems, health issues, or workplace pressures can contribute to interpersonal conflicts.

    5. **Emotional Triggers**: Past traumas, personal sensitivities, or untreated emotional wounds can spark conflict when touched upon, even inadvertently.

Role of Emotions in Conflict:

Emotions play a pivotal role in conflict. While they provide us with insights into our values and needs, unchecked emotions can escalate conflict by creating defensiveness, causing us to misread signals or react without thinking.

Diagram: A flowchart showing:

    • Initial disagreement (two overlapping circles labeled "Differing Views").

- Possible responses: Calm discussion (leading to resolution) or emotional escalation (leading to conflict).

- Emotional escalation can branch off to various sources of conflict (as mentioned above).

Script for Audio Interaction:

Scene: In an office setting, Jamie and Alex have a disagreement about the delegation of tasks.

Jamie: "Alex, why did you take over the Johnson project? I was handling it!"

Alex: (defensively) "You were swamped with work. I thought I was helping!"

Jamie: (irritated) "You should've asked me first. Now it seems like you're trying to take credit for my hard work."

Alex: (raising voice) "That's not fair, Jamie! You always assume the worst. Last time, when I worked overtime, you said I was trying to show you up."

Jamie: (voice shaking) "That's because you always do this. You don't respect me or my work."

Conclusion

The emotional undertones of past grievances and a lack of clear communication escalate the conflict.

Emotions, especially when not understood or regulated, can turn a simple disagreement into a major conflict. By understanding the root causes and being aware of our emotional triggers, we can take steps towards effective conflict management.

Course 9, Section 4

Techniques of Conflict Management and Resolution

Emotional Intelligence-Based Techniques for Conflict Management and Resolution:

1. Self-Awareness and Regulation: Recognizing our own emotions and preventing them from clouding our judgment. This involves taking a step back and reflecting before responding, ensuring that our reactions are constructive.

2. Empathetic Response: Putting oneself in the other person's shoes to truly understand their viewpoint. This doesn't mean agreement, but rather understanding.

3. Open Communication: Speaking clearly and assertively, not aggressively. This involves stating your feelings and needs without attacking the other person.

4. Seeking Win-Win Solutions: Instead of seeing conflict as a competition, approach it collaboratively. Seek solutions that satisfy both parties' needs and interests.

5. Third-Party Mediation: If a resolution can't be reached between the conflicting parties, consider involving a neutral third party to mediate.

Story: "The Overbooked Meeting Room"

In a bustling tech startup, Mia and Raj found themselves in a dilemma. They'd both booked the main conference room for client presentations, and due to a glitch in the booking system, neither received notification of the overlap.

Mia: (anxiously) "Raj, my team's presentation starts in 10 minutes. We've been prepping for weeks!"

Raj: (equally stressed) "Same here, Mia. This is a big account for us. We can't afford to reschedule."

Using her emotional intelligence, Mia took a deep breath, recognizing the rising tension within her. She decided to approach the situation with empathy and understanding.

Mia: "Okay, let's not panic. I understand how crucial this is for you. But it's equally important for us. How can we make this work?"

Raj, taking cue from Mia's calm demeanor, also took a moment to regulate his emotions. "Alright, let's think. We both need a projector and a quiet space. Can we split the presentation locations?"

After a moment of reflection, Mia proposed a win-win solution. "How about this? We take the first half in the conference room and then move to the lounge area for the second half. It's less formal, but it's quiet and has a projector. We'll just have to adjust our presentation style a bit."

Raj agreed, grateful for the compromise. "Sounds good. Thanks, Mia. And after today, let's talk to IT about this glitch. We need to ensure it doesn't happen again."

The conflict, which could have escalated into a heated argument, was handled maturely. Both Mia and Raj demonstrated emotional regulation, empathetic response, and sought a win-win solution to their dilemma.

Conclusion:

By applying emotional intelligence techniques in conflict situations, not only can we find resolutions, but we can also strengthen relationships and foster collaboration.

Course 9, Section 5

Application

Communication and Conflict Management Scenarios

Case Study 1: "Team Deadlines"

Scenario: The marketing team at an e-commerce company is working on a critical project. Lisa, a graphic designer, has been waiting on Alex, the content creator, to deliver his piece so she can complete her designs. Alex, however, is two days late, and the project deadline is fast approaching.

Student Interaction: How should Lisa approach Alex? How can they work together to prevent this from happening in future projects?

Suggested Communication Strategies and Conflict Management Responses:

    1. **Open Communication**: Lisa could start by asking Alex if he faced any challenges or if there's a reason for the delay. By understanding his perspective, she can better gauge the situation.

    2. **Empathetic Response**: Lisa could express understanding and concern for the challenges Alex might be facing while gently reminding him of the team's collective goals.

    3. **Seeking Collaborative Solutions**: Together, they can brainstorm ways to streamline their workflow for future projects, perhaps by setting up interim check-ins or using project management software.

Case Study 2: "Differing Teaching Philosophies"

Scenario: At Greenwood Elementary, two teachers, Mr. Reynolds and Mrs. Patterson, co-teach a mixed-ability class. Mrs. Patterson believes in traditional teaching methods and strict discipline. Mr. Reynolds, however, favors a more interactive and student-led approach. Their differing philosophies are causing friction.

Student Interaction: How can both teachers find a middle ground? What strategies can they use to ensure their teaching methods benefit their students without causing conflict?

Suggested Communication Strategies and Conflict Management Responses:

> 1. **Active Listening**: Both teachers should take the time to actively listen to each other's viewpoints without interruption. They may find that they have more in common than they think.
>
> 2. **Assertive Communication**: They should express their concerns and ideas clearly, stating how they feel their methods benefit the students without belittling each other's philosophies.
>
> 3. **Compromise**: Perhaps they could trial an integrated approach where they merge both their techniques, analyzing student feedback and performance to determine its efficacy.

Case Study 3: "Neighborhood Nuisance"

Scenario: In a quiet suburban neighborhood, the Smiths love hosting weekend parties. They play loud music and often have guests over till the early morning. Their neighbors, the Rodriguez family, are disturbed by the noise, especially as their baby has trouble sleeping.

Student Interaction: How should the Rodriguez family approach the Smiths? What can both families do to ensure harmony in the neighborhood?

Suggested Communication Strategies and Conflict Management Responses:

1. Empathetic Approach: The Rodriguez family could begin by acknowledging the Smiths' love for hosting parties and expressing their concerns about the baby's sleep without sounding accusatory.

2. Seeking Win-Win Solutions: The Rodriguez family might suggest soundproofing solutions or request the Smiths to lower the volume after a certain hour. Alternatively, the Smiths could give the Rodriguez family a heads-up before parties so they can make arrangements.

3. Third-Party Mediation: If direct communication doesn't yield results, they could consider community mediation or involve a neighborhood council to help find a resolution.

Conclusion

In each case, learners should first think of their own approaches and then reflect on the suggested strategies. This interactive process will help hone their communication and conflict management skills in real-world scenarios.

Supplementary Material: Conflict Resolution

The Conflict Resolution Exercise

Jane, an experienced project manager at a tech firm, always prided herself on bringing out the best in her team. Her latest project, however, had her stumped. Two of her most talented team members, Aria and Ethan, were at odds. They were both highly skilled but had different working styles. Aria, the team's lead developer, preferred methodical and detailed planning. Ethan, on the other hand, was the team's creative strategist, often relying on spontaneity and intuition.

One day, during a team meeting, the simmering tension between the two erupted.

"We can't proceed without a clear plan, Ethan!" Aria exclaimed, clearly frustrated. "Your 'let's see where it goes' approach will make us miss our deadline."

Ethan rolled his eyes. "Aria, not everything fits into neat boxes. If we stick only to the 'plan,' we'll never innovate!"

The rest of the team members exchanged uneasy glances. The project's deadline was looming, and the last thing they needed was internal conflict.

Jane decided it was time to step in. She remembered her training in emotional intelligence and recognized the need for effective communication to resolve the conflict.

"Let's take a moment," Jane began, her tone neutral and calming. "Aria, Ethan, I understand both your concerns. Let's break this down."

She continued, "Aria, can you explain why detailed planning is crucial for this phase of the project?"

Aria took a deep breath. "With the coding and testing involved, a structured approach ensures we tackle each aspect efficiently. Without a plan, we risk overlooking critical components."

Jane nodded, then turned to Ethan. "Ethan, can you help us understand your perspective on allowing room for flexibility?"

Ethan hesitated, then replied, "Sure. I believe that while planning is vital, too much rigidity can stifle creativity. Some of our best features came from spontaneous brainstorming. I fear we'll miss such opportunities if we stick solely to the plan."

Jane appreciated their openness. "Both viewpoints are valid," she said. "The key lies in balancing the two. Aria, can you provide a structured outline, and Ethan, could you identify stages where creative input might be most beneficial?"

The two agreed to try. Over the next few days, with Jane facilitating, they developed a hybrid approach. Aria's structured plan ensured every technical aspect was covered, while Ethan introduced "creative checkpoints" – moments in the timeline where the team could brainstorm and innovate.

As the project progressed, Jane noticed a positive shift. Instead of clashing, Aria and Ethan began collaborating, leveraging each other's strengths. Their combined approach led the team to deliver a project that was not only on time but also featured some of the most innovative aspects the company had seen.

Reflecting on the experience, Jane was reminded of the power of emotional intelligence. Recognizing emotions, facilitating open communication, and seeking collaborative solutions had turned a potential disaster into one of the team's biggest successes.

The story was shared across departments as "The Conflict Resolution Exercise," showcasing the benefits of emotional intelligence in the workplace and serving as a testament to the importance of balanced communication and understanding in resolving conflicts effectively.

Parting Thoughts

To reinforce learning, encourage learners to practice the learned communication and conflict management techniques in their daily conversations and reflect on these experiences. This will help them better apply the knowledge gained on this course.

Course 10
Interpersonal Relationships Part 2
Setting Boundaries and Dealing with Difficult People

Learning Objectives for Course 10

1. Understand the role of emotional intelligence in setting and maintaining healthy boundaries in relationships.

2. Learn techniques for setting boundaries and saying no respectfully and assertively.

3. Understand the challenges of dealing with difficult people and how emotional intelligence can help navigate these situations.

4. Learn strategies for dealing with various types of difficult people.

Course 10, Section 1

Understanding Boundaries in Relationships

Definition of Boundaries in Relationships

Boundaries, in the context of relationships, refer to the explicit and implicit limits we establish to protect our well-being, self-worth, and autonomy. These can encompass physical, emotional, mental, and spiritual domains and determine how we allow others to treat us, what we accept, and what we don't. Boundaries can be seen as personal "rules" or guidelines we set for ourselves in interactions with others.

The Importance of Maintaining Healthy Boundaries

1. **Self-preservation and Self-respect**: Setting clear boundaries is a way of demonstrating respect for oneself. It ensures that we don't compromise our values or integrity and that our needs and feelings are considered.

2. **Safety and Protection**: Boundaries create a safe space where individuals can operate without fear of being mistreated or disrespected. This is especially crucial in more intimate relationships.

3. **Preventing Burnout and Resentment**: Consistently compromising one's boundaries can lead to feelings of being taken advantage of, eventually resulting in burnout, resentment, or both.

4. **Enhancing Relationship Quality**: Paradoxically, by setting clear limits, relationships often become more harmonious and satisfying. Both parties understand and respect each other's needs and limits, leading to mutual respect and understanding.

5. **Clarity and Avoiding Misunderstandings**: Clearly communicated boundaries can prevent potential conflicts and misunderstandings in relationships.

Role of Emotional Intelligence in Setting Boundaries

1. **Self-awareness**: The first step in setting boundaries is understanding our own needs, limits, and values. Emotional intelligence helps in recognizing and understanding our own emotions, making it easier to identify when a boundary has been crossed.

2. **Self-regulation**: Once we are aware of our feelings and needs, emotional intelligence equips us with the tools to manage and express those emotions in a constructive manner. This can be especially useful when asserting a boundary that may be challenged or questioned.

3. **Empathy**: While it's essential to prioritize our own needs, it's equally crucial to understand and be sensitive to the emotions of others. Being empathetic can help in explaining our boundaries to others in a way that is compassionate and understanding.

4. **Assertive Communication**: An aspect of emotional intelligence is the ability to communicate our feelings and needs without being aggressive or submissive. This skill is pivotal in setting clear, firm boundaries.

5. **Conflict Resolution**: Even with the clearest communication, boundaries might sometimes lead to disagreements or conflicts. Emotional intelligence aids in navigating these conflicts, ensuring that the boundary is maintained without causing unnecessary strife.

Conclusion:

In summary, boundaries are crucial for individual well-being and the health of a relationship. Emotional intelligence plays a pivotal role in recognizing the need for boundaries, communicating them effectively, and maintaining them even in the face of challenges.

Course 10, Section 2
Setting Boundaries Using Emotional Intelligence

Techniques for Setting Boundaries with Emotional Intelligence

1. **Recognizing One's Own Needs**: This involves self-reflection and honest assessment. It's about identifying what makes you feel comfortable and safe, and what doesn't. Emotional intelligence enables an individual to tune into their emotions, thereby understanding what feels right or wrong for them.

2. **Assertive Communication**: This is the middle ground between aggressive and passive communication. Being assertive means, you express your needs clearly, confidently, and respectfully. It's about saying what you mean, meaning what you say, but not saying it means.

3. **Feedback Loop**: Always be open to feedback. While it's essential to assert your boundaries, it's equally crucial to be receptive to how others feel about them. This ensures mutual respect in any relationship.

4. **Respecting Others' Boundaries**: Just as you wish for your boundaries to be respected, it's essential to do the same for others. Emotional intelligence teaches empathy, which plays a significant role in understanding and respecting the boundaries set by others.

Role-Play Script: Setting Boundaries in a Friendly Relationship

Characters:

- **Alex**: A person who has been feeling overwhelmed and needs some space.

- **Jordan**: Alex's close friend who's unaware of Alex's feelings and is making frequent demands on their time.

Scene opens with Alex and Jordan in a coffee shop. Alex looks a bit tired and overwhelmed.

Jordan: "Hey, Alex! I was thinking we could go watch that new movie tonight, and maybe tomorrow we could hit the beach? Oh, and remember, we have that dinner with the gang on Wednesday!"

Alex: (Takes a deep breath) "Jordan, I truly value our time together, and I appreciate you always wanting to include me in plans. However, lately, I've been feeling a bit overwhelmed with so many activities."

Jordan: "Oh, I didn't realize. What's going on?"

Alex: "It's just a combination of work and personal stuff. I need some time to recharge. Emotional intelligence has taught me to recognize my own needs and to communicate them. I hope you understand."

Jordan: "I wish you'd told me earlier, but I get it. We all need our space. Is there anything I can do?"

Alex: "Thank you for understanding, Jordan. Your support means a lot. Just giving me some time to myself this week would be great. And then we can plan something fun for next week!"

Jordan: "Of course! Let's do that. Always here for you, and thanks for being honest."

Alex: "And thanks for being understanding. This is why our friendship means so much to me."

Scene fades as they continue their conversation, showing a bond strengthened through effective communication and understanding.

Conclusion

The role-play underscores the importance of recognizing one's needs, the art of assertive communication, and mutual respect. Both Alex and Jordan demonstrate emotional intelligence in their conversation, leading to a constructive resolution.

Course 10, Section 3

Dealing with Difficult People - An Overview

Defining "Difficult" in the Context of Relationships:

In the realm of interpersonal relationships, **a "difficult" person** often refers to an individual whose behavior, attitude, or communication style challenges or frustrates others, causing emotional or psychological strain. These individuals may exhibit behaviors that are disruptive, disrespectful, or hurtful. However, it's essential to recognize that labeling someone as "difficult" is subjective. What one person perceives as challenging, another might view as straightforward or even agreeable. As such, understanding and empathy are critical components when dealing with such individuals.

Common Types of Difficult People:

    1. **The Complainer**: Always sees the glass half empty. They continually gripe about their circumstances but rarely take proactive measures to change them.

    2. **The Critic**: They find fault in almost everything and everyone. Their go-to mode is criticism, often without providing constructive feedback.

    3. **The Passive-Aggressive**: While they may not openly express their displeasure or disagreement, their actions subtly convey their true feelings.

    4. **The Know-It-All**: They believe they have the answers to everything and often dismiss others' opinions or feelings.

    5. **The Victim**: They perpetually feel the world is against them and shirk responsibility for their actions, always placing the blame on external factors.

    6. **The Attention Seeker**: Craves validation and recognition and might use dramatic tales or exaggerated situations to remain in the spotlight.

    7. **The Negative Nellie**: Always focuses on the downside of situations, often sapping the energy and optimism from group dynamics.

Imagination Infographic

Types of Difficult People & Their Characteristics

Format: A circular diagram divided into seven equal parts (like a pie chart), each segment representing one type of difficult person.

1. The Complainer

    - **Image**: A cloud with rain.
    - **Caption**: "Always seeing the negative side."

2. The Critic

    - **Image**: A magnifying glass highlighting a minor flaw.
    - **Caption**: "Finding fault in everything."

3. The Passive-Aggressive

    - **Image**: A smiling mask with a frown behind it.
    - **Caption**: "Hidden displeasure."

4. The Know-It-All

    - **Image**: A person on a podium with others silenced.
    - **Caption**: "Dismisses others' views."

5. The Victim

    - **Image**: A puppet on strings.
    - **Caption**: "Externalizes blame."

6. The Attention Seeker

    - **Image**: A spotlight on a single person on stage.
    - **Caption**: "Needs to be center stage."

7. The Negative Nellie

    - **Image**: A half-empty glass.
    - **Caption**: "Always pessimistic."

At the center of the circular diagram, there's a caption: **"Understanding and Empathy are Key."**

Conclusion:

Understanding these various **"difficult"** personas can empower individuals with the knowledge and strategies needed to interact with them effectively. Moreover, recognizing these traits can also help us introspect and rectify any similar behaviors we may unknowingly exhibit.

Course 10, Section 4
Using Emotional Intelligence to Navigate Difficult Interactions

Understanding and effectively managing interactions with difficult individuals is crucial for personal and professional success. Emotional intelligence (EI) equips us with the tools and skills needed to navigate these challenging waters. Let's delve into specific strategies for dealing with various difficult personalities and how EI plays a pivotal role in each.

1. **Passive Aggressive**:

Understanding: Recognize that their behavior often stems from an inability or unwillingness to express feelings openly. Their aggression is "passive" and may manifest in avoidance, procrastination, or backhanded compliments.

Emotional Intelligence Strategy:

- **Self-awareness**: Recognize and manage your own reactions to passive-aggressive behavior.

- **Empathy**: Understand that passive aggression might arise from fear of direct confrontation.

- **Assertive Communication**: Address the behavior directly but non-confrontationally, asking open-ended questions to encourage open communication.

2. **Narcissists**:

Understanding: Narcissists often have a heightened sense of self-importance, a deep need for admiration, and a lack of empathy for others.

Emotional Intelligence Strategy:

- **Self-regulation**: Manage your emotions and avoid being baited into an emotional outburst.

- **Empathy**: Understand that behind the facade, narcissists often deal with issues related to self-worth.

- **Boundaries**: Set clear boundaries and stick to them. It's essential to protect yourself emotionally.

3. Chronically Negative Individuals:

Understanding: Constant negativity can be exhausting. These individuals often struggle with an ingrained negative mindset, viewing situations from a pessimistic perspective.

Emotional Intelligence Strategy:

- **Self-awareness**: Recognize your feelings when interacting with them and ensure they don't affect your mood.

- **Empathy**: Understand that chronic negativity might stem from past experiences or deep-seated fears.

- **Positive Reinforcement**: Encourage and reinforce positive behaviors and comments. Offer a different perspective while acknowledging their feelings.

Emotional Intelligence: The Key to Navigating Difficult Interactions

1. **Self-awareness**: Recognizing our own emotional reactions allows us to approach situations more objectively. When we're aware of how we feel, we can manage our responses better.

2. **Self-regulation**: Being in control of our emotions means not letting the negative behavior of others dictate our emotional state.

3. **Motivation**: Being driven by a purpose or goal, rather than reactive emotional responses, can help steer conversations in a constructive direction.

4. **Empathy**: Understanding where someone is coming from, even if you don't agree, can pave the way for more productive interactions.

5. **Social Skills**: Effective communication and interpersonal effectiveness can defuse potential conflicts and foster understanding.

Conclusion:

In essence, dealing with difficult people is a test of one's emotional intelligence. The ability to stay calm, communicate effectively, and maintain a sense of empathy even in trying situations showcases strong EI and leads to more fulfilling interpersonal relationships.

Course 10, Section 5

Application: Boundaries and Difficult People Scenarios

1. Scenario: The Complainer

Background: Every team meeting, Maria brings up the same issues, focusing solely on problems without ever offering solutions.

Question for Learners: How would you address Maria's repetitive complaints and channel her energy towards proactive problem-solving?

Potential Approaches:

> 1. **Problem-Solution Format**: Encourage a format where every complaint must be paired with a potential solution.
>
> 2. **Acknowledge and Redirect**: Acknowledge Maria's concerns and direct her towards collaborative problem-solving.
>
> 3. **Private Discussion**: Engage Maria in a one-on-one chat to understand the root of her complaints and guide her towards a more constructive approach.

2. Scenario: The Critic

Background: Jason meticulously points out even minor mistakes in projects, often overshadowing the overall success of the work.

Question for Learners: How can you ensure a balanced feedback approach from Jason without suppressing his attention to detail?

Potential Approaches:

> 1. **Feedback Sandwich**: Introduce the concept of starting with a positive comment, followed by criticism, and ending with another positive remark.
>
> 2. **Scope Limitation**: Encourage Jason to prioritize feedback, focusing on major issues rather than inconsequential details.

3. **Constructive Criticism Training**: Offer or suggest training sessions or materials on providing constructive feedback.

3. Scenario: The Passive-Aggressive

Background: Lucy often agrees to tasks verbally but displays resentment through her actions or lack of timely completion.

Question for Learners: How can you address Lucy's passive-aggressive behavior and promote open communication?

Potential Approaches:

1. **Open-Ended Questions**: Proactively ask Lucy how she feels about tasks or if she foresees any challenges.

2. **Clear Expectations**: Define clear expectations and timelines, checking in periodically.

. **Feedback Session**: Create an environment where Lucy feels safe to express any reservations or concerns directly.

4. Scenario: The Know-It-All

Background: During brainstorming sessions, Derek often dismisses others' ideas, believing his solutions are superior.

Question for Learners: How can you foster a collaborative environment where Derek and others feel equally valued?

Potential Approaches:

1. **Group Validation**: Encourage all team members to share feedback on presented ideas.

2. **Idea Voting**: Let the team vote on solutions anonymously, promoting fairness.

3. **Rotational Leadership**: Rotate the lead role in brainstorming sessions to diversify the approach.

5. Scenario: The Victim

Background: Whenever a project encounters challenges, Anna tends to externalize blame and never acknowledges her role in the setbacks.

Question for Learners: How can you help Anna take accountability without feeling targeted?

Potential Approaches:

>1. **Reflective Feedback**: Frame feedback in a way that encourages self-reflection, e.g., "How do you think we could have approached this differently?"

>2. **Collaborative Review**: Encourage team post-mortems after projects to discuss what went well and areas of improvement collectively.

>3. **Skill Development**: Recommend training or resources that foster accountability and proactive problem-solving.

6. Scenario: The Attention Seeker

Background: In team meetings, Chris frequently diverts the topic to discuss his achievements, sometimes overshadowing others.

Question for Learners: How can you ensure that everyone gets a chance to shine without undermining Chris's achievements?

Potential Approaches:

>1. **Structured Sharing**: Allocate specific times for team members to share personal achievements, ensuring everyone gets a turn.

>2. **Agenda-Driven Meetings**: Stick to a pre-defined agenda to ensure topic deviations are minimized.

>3. **Private Acknowledgment**: Recognize Chris's achievements privately, reducing his need to seek validation during group settings.

7. Scenario: The Negative Nellie

Background: No matter the success rate of projects, Elise always anticipates failure and frequently voices her pessimistic outlook.

Question for Learners: How can you promote a positive work environment without invalidating Elise's concerns?

Potential Approaches:

1. **Positivity Training**: Introduce resources or training on maintaining a positive outlook, emphasizing its impact on performance.

2. **Success Celebrations**: Regularly celebrate team successes, no matter how small, to reinforce positive outcomes.

3. **Constructive Discussions**: Encourage Elise to voice her concerns in a constructive manner, focusing on potential solutions rather than mere problems.

Conclusion:

Emotional intelligence plays a crucial role in navigating relationships with various personalities in a work environment. Recognizing, understanding, and effectively dealing with different behaviors can foster a harmonious and productive team atmosphere.

Supplementary Material: Boundary Setting in An Interactive Story

The Boundary Setter

Setting: A busy corporate office.

Introduction: You've recently been promoted to team lead for a project. Your excitement is palpable. However, as you start working with your team, you quickly realize that it's not just about managing work but also personalities. You recall Lesson 10 from your emotional intelligence curriculum and feel equipped to set boundaries and deal with the varied personalities you encounter.

Interaction 1: The Meeting with The Complainer

Maria constantly emphasizes the project's potential challenges without suggesting any solutions.

>**Option A**: Let her vent, hoping she feels heard and moves on.
>
>**Option B**: Directly ask her for potential solutions to the challenges she's highlighting.
>
>**Option C**: Address it outside the meeting to avoid a confrontational situation.
>
>-------------------
>
>If **Option A**: Maria feels heard but continues with her pattern in subsequent meetings.
>
>If **Option B**: Maria realizes the need for a constructive approach and starts brainstorming solutions.
>
>If **Option C**: Maria appreciates the private feedback and makes an effort to be solution oriented.

Interaction 2: Feedback Session with The Critic

Jason sends you a detailed email, nitpicking minor mistakes in the project.

>**Option A**: Defensively point out the overall success of the project.
>
>**Option B**: Thank him for his feedback and ask for a meeting to discuss prioritized concerns.
>
>**Option C**: Ignore the email, hoping he takes the hint.
>
>-------------------
>
>**If Option A**: Jason feels unheard and becomes even more critical.
>
>**If Option B**: In the meeting, both of you arrive at a balanced feedback approach.
>
>**If Option C**: Jason feels ignored and starts sharing his criticisms with team members, causing unrest.

Interaction 3: Delegating Tasks to The Passive-Aggressive

Lucy agrees to take on a task, but you notice her subtle cues of displeasure.

>**Option A**: Pretend you didn't notice and hope for the best.
>
>**Option B**: Ask her openly if she has reservations.
>
>**Option C**: Delegate the task to someone else to avoid potential conflict.
>
>-------------------
>
>**If Option A**: The task isn't completed on time, leading to project delays.
>
>**If Option B**: Lucy admits her discomfort, allowing you to address her concerns or reallocate the task.
>
>**If Option C**: Lucy feels bypassed and becomes more passive-aggressive in future interactions.

Interaction 4: Brainstorming with The Know-It-All

Derek dismisses another team member's idea during a brainstorming session.

    Option A: Challenge his idea to level the playing field.

    Option B: Ask others for their opinions to promote a democratic discussion.

    Option C: Let Derek take charge, hoping it'll ensure a successful project.

    If Option A: Derek becomes defensive, causing a heated argument.

    If Option B: The team feels valued, and Derek realizes the importance of collaborative thinking.

    If Option C: Team members feel unheard, leading to low morale.

Interaction 5: Post-Project Review with The Victim

Anna blames external factors for her tasks not meeting the deadline.

    Option A: Highlight areas where the team succeeded in shifting focus.

    Option B: Ask open-ended questions to make Anna self-reflect.

    Option C: Confront her about the missed deadlines.

    If Option A: Anna continues her victim mentality in future projects.

    If Option B: Anna introspects and acknowledges areas of improvement.

    If Option C: Anna feels targeted and becomes defensive.

Interaction 6: Presentation Preparation with The Attention Seeker

Chris keeps sharing his achievements during team preparation for an important presentation.

Option A: Allocate specific slots for each person to share insights.

Option B: Acknowledge his achievements and then steer him back to the agenda.

Option C: Allow him to dominate, hoping his enthusiasm will benefit the presentation.

If Option A: The preparation goes smoothly with everyone feeling valued.

If Option B: Chris feels acknowledged but learns the importance of staying on track.

If Option C: Team members feel overshadowed, and the presentation lacks a cohesive approach.

Interaction 7: Project Kick-off with The Negative Nellie

Elise shares her pessimistic outlook on the new project's prospects.

Option A: Challenge her views and promote optimism.

Option B: Ask her for constructive feedback to be better prepared.

Option C: Dismiss her concerns to maintain a positive atmosphere.

If Option A: Elise feels targeted and retreats, becoming even more negative.

If Option B: Elise's concerns help the team prepare better, making her feel valued.

If Option C: The team misses out on potential pitfalls, leading to issues down the line.

Conclusion

The project progresses with its ups and downs. How you dealt with each personality type determines the overall success of the project and the team's morale. You realize the invaluable role of emotional intelligence in managing team dynamics and fostering a positive and productive environment.

Summary

This story demonstrates that each decision has consequences. Emotional intelligence helps navigate the complexities of interpersonal relationships, leading to more harmonious and productive outcomes.

Parting Thoughts

Remember to include activities for reflection after each section and encourage learners to apply these techniques in real life for more effective learning.

Course 11

Interpersonal Relationships Part 3

Navigating Complex Social Situations and Maintaining Healthy Relationships

Learning Objectives for Course 11

1. Understand how emotional intelligence can guide us in complex social situations.

2. Learn techniques for navigating intricate social contexts, like workplace politics, multicultural environments, or challenging family dynamics.

3. Understand the role of emotional intelligence in maintaining healthy relationships over time.

4. Learn strategies for maintaining relationship health, such as regular check-ins, active listening, and expressing appreciation.

Course 11, Section 1

Understanding Complex Social Situations

What is a Complex Social Situation?

A **complex social situation** refers to an interaction or series of interactions characterized by multiple layers of interpersonal dynamics, often involving conflicting emotions, interests, or values. These situations can be spontaneous or anticipated, short-lived or prolonged. Complexity can arise from the number of people involved, the nature of the relationship(s), cultural or societal expectations, or the particular circumstances surrounding the situation.

Characteristics of Complex Social Situations:

    1. **Ambiguity**: These situations often lack clarity. The 'right' behavior or response might not be readily apparent, leading to uncertainty.

    2. **Diverse Perspectives**: Multiple individuals might have differing viewpoints, beliefs, or interests.

    3. **Emotional Intensity**: High stakes, either personal or professional, can elevate emotions and tensions.

    4. **Unpredictability**: The outcome of the situation can be uncertain, and the reaction of individuals can vary.

    5. **Interpersonal Dependencies**: Actions or decisions by one individual can significantly affect others in the scenario.

Challenges Posed by Complex Social Situations:

    1. **Stress and Anxiety**: The intricacy of the situation can be mentally taxing, leading to increased stress.

    2. **Miscommunication**: With multiple layers of interpersonal dynamics, there's a high risk of misunderstanding or misinterpreting information.

3. **Potential for Conflict**: The amalgamation of different perspectives can lead to disagreements or outright conflicts.

4. **Decision Paralysis**: The fear of making the wrong move can sometimes hinder any move at all.

5. **Relationship Strains**: If not navigated well, these situations can strain or break personal or professional relationships.

6. **Cultural or Social Missteps**: Especially in diverse settings, there's potential to unintentionally offend or misstep.

Importance of Recognizing Complex Social Situations:

Recognizing the complexity of a social situation is the first step in addressing it. Awareness allows individuals to approach the situation with sensitivity, preparedness, and adaptability. It paves the way for proactive thinking, where one can strategize about the best ways to navigate the situation while maintaining respect and understanding for all involved.

Conclusion:

Complex social situations, while challenging, are an inevitable part of human interactions. They test our emotional intelligence, adaptability, and interpersonal skills. By understanding their nature and the challenges they present, individuals can better equip themselves to navigate these scenarios with grace, understanding, and efficacy. The subsequent sections of this lesson will delve deeper into strategies and tools to address these situations effectively.

Course 11, Section 2

Navigating Complex Social Situations with Emotional Intelligence

Introduction:

Emotional intelligence is the capacity to recognize, understand, and manage our own emotions while also being attuned to the emotions of others. Using emotional intelligence as a navigational tool in complex social situations can lead to better outcomes, smoother interactions, and preserved relationships. Here's how the principles of emotional intelligence can be applied.

Techniques for Managing Complex Social Situations:

1. **Self-awareness**:

- **Definition**: Recognizing and understanding one's own emotions.

- **Application**: Before reacting in any situation, take a moment to identify and understand your emotions. This self-reflection can prevent unnecessary outbursts or conflicts.

2. **Empathy**:

- **Definition**: Understanding and sharing the feelings of another.

- **Application**: Put yourself in the shoes of others involved in the situation. This allows you to gauge their emotional state and respond more thoughtfully.

3. **Assertiveness**:

- **Definition**: Expressing one's opinions and desires in a confident yet respectful manner.

- **Application**: Stand up for your beliefs and feelings without violating the boundaries of others. This ensures that your voice is heard without triggering defensive reactions.

4. **Perspective-taking**:

> • **Definition**: Considering a situation or issue from another person's viewpoint.
>
> • **Application**: When multiple viewpoints exist, trying to understand all sides can reduce miscommunication and conflict.

5. **Emotional Regulation**:

> • **Definition**: The ability to control one's emotions, especially in stressful situations.
>
> • **Application**: In charged scenarios, stay calm and think before responding. This can prevent escalation and lead to more rational decisions.

6. **Active Listening**:

> • **Definition**: Listening attentively without interrupting and giving feedback when appropriate.
>
> • **Application**: Truly hear what others are saying. This not only provides clarity but also makes others feel valued.

Infographic

Title: "Navigating Social Complexity with Emotional Intelligence"

> **Visual 1**: A brain with different colored sections representing emotions.
>
>> • **Label**: "Self-awareness"
>>
>> • **Caption**: "Tune in to your emotions before reacting."
>
> **Visual 2**: Two shoes, with one being in the other's position.
>
>> • **Label**: "Empathy"
>>
>> • **Caption**: "Feel what others feel."
>
> **Visual 3**: A figure standing tall yet with an open hand extended forward.
>
>> • **Label**: "Assertiveness"
>>
>> • **Caption**: "Speak up but remain respectful."

Visual 4: An eye looking at different angles or perspectives.

- **Label**: "Perspective-taking"
- **Caption**: "See from all sides."

Visual 5: A thermometer with a calm, medium, and agitated state.

- **Label**: "Emotional Regulation"
- **Caption**: "Stay cool under pressure."

Visual 6: An ear with sound waves, emphasizing focus.

- **Label**: "Active Listening"
- **Caption**: "Hear and understand fully."

Conclusion

Complex social situations demand nuanced handling. Leveraging emotional intelligence offers a structured, effective approach to navigate these scenarios, leading to healthier interactions and stronger relationships.

Course 11, Section 3

Maintaining Healthy Relationships - An Overview

Introduction

Healthy relationships, whether platonic, familial, or romantic, are foundational to our well-being. They provide support, love, and a sense of belonging. But what exactly makes a relationship healthy? And how can emotional intelligence play a role in maintaining it?

Characteristics of Healthy Relationships:

1. **Mutual Respect**: Both parties value and honor each other's boundaries, opinions, and feelings.

2. **Trust**: Essential for the security of a relationship. It means believing that the other person will act with integrity and honesty.

3. **Open Communication**: Being able to express oneself without fear and listening actively to the other.

4. **Compromise**: Finding common ground when disagreements arise, where both parties can feel satisfied.

5. **Independence**: Both parties have their own interests, friends, and activities, and they support each other in pursuing them.

6. **Support**: Being there for one another, not just in happy times, but especially during challenges.

7. **Honesty**: Being truthful and transparent, which strengthens the foundation of trust.

8. **Equality**: Both parties have equal say and value each other's input.

The Role of Emotional Intelligence in Maintaining Healthy Relationships:

1. **Self-awareness**: Recognizing one's emotions prevents projecting negative feelings onto a partner or friend.

2. **Empathy**: Helps in understanding the emotions and needs of the other person, fostering deeper connection and mutual understanding.

3. **Effective Communication**: Leveraging active listening and thoughtful response ensures misunderstandings are minimized.

4. **Emotional Regulation**: By managing one's emotions, conflicts can be resolved more calmly and rationally.

5. **Social Skills**: Facilitates better interactions and understanding of social dynamics, leading to smoother relationship management.

Imagination Infographic

Title: "Building Blocks of Healthy Relationships"

Visual 1: Two hands holding, symbolizing unity.

- **Label**: "Mutual Respect"
- **Caption**: "Valuing each other's boundaries."

Visual 2: A locked heart.

- **Label**: "Trust"
- **Caption**: "The foundation of any relationship."

Visual 3: Two figures, one speaking with the other actively listening.

- **Label**: "Open Communication"
- **Caption**: "Speak, listen, understand."

Visual 4: Two puzzle pieces fitting together.

- **Label**: "Compromise"
- **Caption**: "Finding the middle ground."

Visual 5: Two figures standing side by side, with individual interests shown in thought bubbles.

- **Label**: "Independence"
- **Caption**: "Together, yet individual."

Visual 6: One figure supporting another, lifting them up.

- **Label**: "Support"
- **Caption**: "Being there at all times."

Visual 7: An open book.

- **Label**: "Honesty"
- **Caption**: "Transparency strengthens trust."

Visual 8: A balanced scale.

- **Label**: "Equality"
- **Caption**: "Equal say, equal respect."

Conclusion

Healthy relationships thrive on mutual respect, open communication, and a sense of equality. Emotional intelligence acts as the bridge that supports and strengthens these foundational elements, ensuring relationships remain fulfilling and enduring.

Course 11, Section 4

Strategies for Maintaining Healthy Relationships

1. Regular Communication

Introduction: Regular communication is about ensuring that you're staying connected by routinely checking in with one another, discussing daily events, and sharing feelings or concerns.

Role Play Script:

Scene: A living room. JAMES is reading a book. LUCY sits beside him.

Lucy: "Hey, how was your meeting with the new client today?"

James: "Oh, it was good. We managed to finalize the contract. Thanks for asking. How was your day?"

Lucy: "It was hectic, but I had a great conversation with Sarah about the project we're working on."

James: "That's good to hear. Let's make it a point to catch up like this every evening. It helps me feel more connected to you."

Lucy: "I agree. Sharing these moments matters."

2. Active Listening

Introduction: Active listening is about fully concentrating, understanding, and responding to what the other person is saying, without interrupting or letting your mind wander.

Role Play Script:

Scene: Coffee shop. ANNA is visibly upset. MIA is across the table from her.

Anna: "I had a disagreement with my boss today. It just felt so overwhelming."

Mia (nodding): "That sounds tough. Tell me more about what happened."

Anna: "Well, he didn't understand the perspective I was coming from. It felt like he wasn't even trying."

Mia: "It must have been frustrating to feel unheard. What did you do next?"

3. Conflict Resolution

Introduction: Conflict resolution involves understanding and resolving disagreements in a constructive manner, focusing on the problem at hand rather than attacking each other.

Role Play Script:

Scene: Kitchen. BEN spills milk. EMILY sighs loudly.

Ben: "I know I'm clumsy sometimes. I'm sorry."

Emily: "It's not just about the milk, Ben. I've been feeling like I'm handling most of the chores."

Ben: "Let's talk about it. How can we divide the tasks more fairly?"

Emily: "I'd appreciate that. Maybe we can create a chore chart?"

Ben: "That sounds like a plan. Let's work on it together."

4. Expressing Gratitude

Introduction: Gratitude is about acknowledging and appreciating the actions, efforts, or qualities of the other person, reinforcing positive feelings and affirming the relationship.

Role Play Script:

Scene: A balcony with sunset view. KATE hands JASON a cup of tea.

Jason: "This is perfect. Just the way I like it. Thank you."

Kate: "I'm glad you like it. And thank you for helping with the kids' homework today. It gave me a much-needed break."

Jason: "Always here to help. I appreciate all you do for us, Kate."

Kate: "It's a team effort. Thank you for being a great partner."

Conclusion

Maintaining healthy relationships is an ongoing endeavor. It's built on a series of moments—moments of understanding, appreciation, and genuine connection. The strategies highlighted are tools to facilitate these moments, creating relationships that are both resilient and fulfilling.

Course 11, Section 5

Application: Complex Social Situations and Relationship Maintenance Scenarios

Introduction:

Leverage these real-life scenarios to check your understanding of how to maintain relationships with emotional intelligence in complex situations. There are discussion points following each scenario to guide your thought processes. You may want to refer back to the 6 techniques for managing complex social situations from the beginning of this lesson for inspiration. They are self-awareness, empathy, assertiveness, perspective-taking, emotional regulation, and active listening.

Scenario 1: The Surprise Guest

Setting: Alex's house party.

Background: Alex has invited Sam to the party, forgetting that Taylor, Sam's ex, is also on the guest list. When Sam arrives, the surprise of seeing Taylor creates tension in the room.

Task for Learners: How should Alex navigate this situation? How can Sam manage the sudden discomfort of unexpectedly running into an ex?

Discussion Points:

- The importance of empathy and understanding in unexpected situations.
- Techniques for de-escalation and making amends.
- Finding common ground in awkward situations.

Scenario 2: Workplace Dynamics

Setting: Corporate office break room.

Background: Jordan, a mid-level manager, has been struggling to communicate with Chris, an employee, over project expectations. They both ran into each other during a coffee break. The air is thick with unspoken grievances.

Task for Learners: How can Jordan open up a conversation about the project without making Chris defensive? How can Chris express his concerns while still showing respect for Jordan's position?

Discussion Points:

- The role of active listening in addressing workplace concerns.
- Importance of non-confrontational feedback.
- Ways to ensure mutual understanding and respect in communication.

Scenario 3: Family Ties

Setting: Sunday family lunch at Grandma's house.

Background: Every Sunday, Emily has lunch with her large family. Lately, political discussions have been causing rifts between family members with different views. Emily wants everyone to get along but doesn't want to suppress meaningful conversations.

Task for Learners: How can Emily create a space where everyone feels heard and respected, even when they disagree?

Discussion Points:

- The significance of setting boundaries in family discussions.
- Techniques to redirect or diffuse potentially explosive conversations.
- Understanding that it's okay to 'agree to disagree'.

Scenario 4: Long-Distance Relationship Challenges

Setting: A Skype call between Lee and Jamie.

Background: Lee and Jamie have been in a long-distance relationship for a year. Lately, they've been feeling disconnected due to different time zones and schedules. They've set up this call to address the issue.

Task for Learners: How can both Lee and Jamie express their feelings, understand each other's challenges, and work towards a solution?

Discussion Points:

- The importance of regular communication in maintaining connection.
- Balancing individual needs with relationship needs.
- Creative ways to stay connected and cultivate intimacy from a distance.

Scenario 5: Community Conflicts

Setting: Neighborhood community meeting.

Background: Residents are divided over a proposed high-rise development in their suburban community. Some see it as an opportunity for growth, while others believe it will ruin the neighborhood's charm. Clara, a long-time resident, wants to bridge the divide.

Task for Learners: How can Clara facilitate a productive conversation between opposing sides?

Discussion Points:

- The value of perspective-taking in understanding different viewpoints.
- Techniques for encouraging civil discourse.
- Finding compromise and seeking win-win solutions.

Conclusion

Each of these scenarios provides a unique challenge that can be addressed with the principles of emotional intelligence. By actively practicing in these situations, learners can hone their skills and apply them in real-life situations to foster understanding and harmony.

Supplementary Material: Navigating Complex Social Situations

Navigating the Maze

Scene 1: The Office Gathering

[Animation/Text Description: An office space decorated with balloons. A sign reads "Happy Retirement, Mr. Thompson!" Colleagues are chatting, and there's a general feeling of festivity.]

Narrator: You're at a retirement party for Mr. Thompson, your boss of five years. As you scan the room, you spot two groups. One consists of your close office friends, and the other, senior management, which includes Jane, who you've had misunderstandings within the past.

Decision Point:

    1. Join your close friends and have a good time.

    2. Approach the senior management group and try to mend bridges with Jane.

If Decision 1:

Narrator: You have a fun evening laughing and recalling memories. But did you miss an opportunity to resolve past differences with Jane?

If Decision 2:

Narrator: Jane seems surprised but appreciates the gesture. You both have a meaningful conversation and decide to start afresh. This could be the start of a more harmonious working relationship.

Scene 2: Family Dinner Drama

[Animation/Text Description: A cozy dining room. Family members are seated around the table, plates full. Conversations are in full swing.]

Narrator: At a family dinner, your cousin starts discussing politics, a topic that's caused arguments before. You can sense the tension rising.

Decision Point:

    1. Stay silent and hope the topic changes.

    2. Steer the conversation towards a more neutral topic.

    3. Address the elephant in the room and suggest avoiding controversial topics at family gatherings.

If Decision 1:

Narrator: The evening progresses without major confrontations, but there's an undercurrent of unease throughout.

If Decision 2:

Narrator: You ask about the latest family trip, effectively diverting attention. The mood lightens, and the rest of the dinner goes off without a hitch.

If Decision 3:

Narrator: There's a brief silence, but then others nod in agreement. It's acknowledged that family gatherings are for bonding and not for disagreements. The air clears, and the evening continues harmoniously.

Scene 3: Friends Falling Apart

[Animation/Text Description: A cafe with two friends seated across from each other. One seems upset.]

Narrator: You meet your friend, Alex, for coffee. Lately, you've felt a distance growing between you two. Today, Alex seems particularly withdrawn.

Decision Point:

    1. Ignore the vibe and chat about general topics.

    2. Ask Alex directly if something's wrong.

    3. Share your feelings of distance and ask for Alex's perspective.

If Decision 1:

Narrator: The meeting ends on a polite note, but the distance between you two feels even more pronounced.

If Decision 2:

Narrator: Alex looks taken aback but then admits to going through personal issues. You feel closer, understanding the reason behind Alex's behavior.

If Decision 3:

Narrator: Alex appreciates your honesty and opens up about feeling left out when you missed their birthday for a work commitment. You both discuss your feelings and find ways to strengthen your bond.

Conclusion:

Narrator: Navigating social situations, especially complex ones, is akin to moving through a maze. Each decision can lead to a different outcome. The key is to be mindful, understand the context, and use emotional intelligence to create meaningful, positive interactions.

[End with an Animation or Text Description: The maze from the beginning now displays a clear path, symbolizing the learner's journey through complex situations.]

Parting Thought

As with the other courses, make sure to include reflective activities after each section and encourage learners to apply these strategies and techniques in their daily lives.

Course 12
Emotional Intelligence in the Workplace
Part 1
Teamwork and Collaboration

Learning Objectives for Course 12

1. Understand the role of emotional intelligence in teamwork and collaboration within a workplace setting.

2. Learn techniques to enhance teamwork through emotional intelligence, such as empathetic communication and effective conflict resolution.

3. Recognize the benefits of emotionally intelligent teamwork to individual and organizational success.

Course 12, Section 1

Introduction to Emotional Intelligence in Teamwork

Emotional intelligence (EI) can be described as the ability to recognize, understand, manage, and effectively express one's own emotions, as well as the ability to engage and navigate successfully with the emotions of others. In a workplace setting, where diverse personalities and roles converge, emotional intelligence becomes even more crucial, especially when it comes to teamwork and collaboration.

1. **The Dynamics of Teamwork**:

Teams are the lifeblood of most modern organizations. They consist of individuals from various backgrounds, cultures, and temperaments, all working towards a common goal. However, the success of these teams isn't solely based on individual skills and talents but also on how well these individuals work together.

2. **The Role of Emotional Intelligence in Team Cohesion**:

- **Self-Awareness**: Recognizing one's own emotions and their effects can help individuals understand their strengths and limitations, paving the way for open communication and allowing team members to lean on each other's strengths.

- **Self-Management**: The ability to manage disruptive emotions and impulses is crucial in a team setting. Those who can stay composed, positive, and unflappable even in challenging situations can inspire the same in their teammates.

- **Empathy**: Understanding the emotions of team members can foster a supportive environment. Recognizing when a colleague is feeling stressed, overwhelmed, or demotivated and offering support can build trust and strengthen team cohesion.

- **Interpersonal Effectiveness**: Building bonds, nurturing instrumental relationships, and expressing oneself clearly are all components of EI that can smooth out potential frictions in a team, leading to efficient collaboration.

3. Enhanced Collaboration Through Emotional Intelligence:

When team members practice emotional intelligence, they cultivate a workspace that values:

- Open Communication: Openness encourages team members to share ideas without fear of judgment, leading to more innovative solutions.

- Mutual Respect: Recognizing and valuing the emotions of others can reduce conflicts and misunderstandings.

- Trust: Teams that trust each other can work faster and more efficiently as they are confident in each other's capabilities and intentions.

- Adaptability: Emotionally intelligent teams are better equipped to handle change, as they can understand and manage the emotional undertones of transitions.

4. The Bigger Picture:

In the grand scheme of organizational goals, emotionally intelligent teams are more agile, resilient, and adaptable. They can navigate challenges with ease, celebrate each other's successes, and collectively learn from failures. As organizations recognize the importance of EI, investing in training and development in this area is no longer a luxury but a necessity. After all, organizations thrive when their teams do, and teams excel when emotional intelligence is at their core.

Conclusion

In conclusion, as the workplace continues to evolve, with increasing emphasis on teamwork and collaboration, emotional intelligence stands out as a foundational skill set that can significantly enhance team dynamics, productivity, and overall workplace satisfaction.

Course 12, Section 2

Techniques to Enhance Teamwork Using Emotional Intelligence

Emotional intelligence plays a vital role in enhancing teamwork in the workplace. When employed effectively, EI techniques can lead to harmonious work environments, bolster productivity, and foster innovation. Below are some key techniques rooted in emotional intelligence that can be harnessed to enhance teamwork:

1. **Empathetic Communication**:

Definition: Empathetic communication is about truly understanding and sharing the feelings of another. It involves active listening, validation, and a non-judgmental approach.

Application:

- **Active Listening**: This involves fully concentrating, understanding, and responding to what the other person is saying, rather than formulating a reply while they're still speaking.

- **Validation**: Acknowledging the feelings and perspectives of team members, even if you don't necessarily agree. This creates a sense of value and respect.

- **Open-ended Questions**: Asking questions that require more than a 'yes' or 'no' answer encourages deeper conversations and shows that you are genuinely interested in understanding.

2. **Effective Conflict Resolution**:

Definition: Conflict is inevitable in any team setting. Effective conflict resolution is about addressing disputes in a manner that is constructive and promotes mutual understanding.

Application:

- **Stay Calm and Composed**: Reacting emotionally can escalate conflicts. Taking deep breaths, taking a break, or practicing mindfulness can help in managing one's reactions.

- **Seek First to Understand**: Before presenting your point of view, ensure you fully understand the other person's perspective.

- **Focus on the Issue, Not the Person**: Address the issue at hand without getting personal or making attacks.

- **Seek Win-Win Solutions**: Look for solutions where all parties feel they have gained something or at least haven't lost anything significant.

3. **Shared Emotional Understanding**:

Definition: This refers to a collective sense of understanding emotions within a team, where team members are attuned to each other's emotional states and respond accordingly.

Application:

- Regular Check-ins: Taking time to discuss not just work but also how team members are feeling can cultivate an emotionally supportive environment.

- Emotional Vocabulary: Encouraging the use of a rich emotional vocabulary can help in expressing feelings more accurately. For instance, instead of just saying "I'm fine," one might say, "I'm feeling a bit overwhelmed but hopeful."

- Create a Safe Space: Cultivate an environment where team members feel safe to express their emotions without fear of retribution or ridicule.

4. **Celebrate Achievements and Learn from Failures**:

Definition: Recognizing successes and taking failures as learning opportunities, rather than points of blame.

Application:

- Group Recognition: Celebrate team achievements, whether big or small, to foster a sense of collective accomplishment.

- Constructive Feedback: Instead of placing blame, focus on what can be learned from setbacks. Encourage a growth mindset.

5. Encourage Perspective-Taking:

Definition: The act of viewing situations from another's point of view.

Application:

- Role Reversal Exercises: Occasionally let team members swap roles or responsibilities to understand the challenges faced by their peers.

- Encourage Diverse Thinking: Embrace and encourage diverse opinions and perspectives as they can lead to richer solutions and broader understanding.

Conclusion:

In summary, enhancing teamwork using emotional intelligence involves recognizing emotions (both our own and others'), understanding their impact, and using this knowledge to foster a more cohesive and effective team environment. With these techniques, teams can navigate challenges more smoothly, harness the power of collective intelligence, and achieve shared goals.

Course 12, Section 3

The Benefits of Emotionally Intelligent Teamwork

Emotionally Intelligent (EI) teamwork holds transformative power for both the individuals involved and the organization they're part of. When teams operate with a high degree of emotional intelligence, they tap into benefits that go beyond the immediate tasks at hand. Here's a deeper look at some of these advantages:

1. Increased Productivity:

> • **Emotionally Balanced Decision Making**: Teams with high EI tend to make decisions based on a mix of logic and emotion. This balance prevents rash decisions that can arise from high-stress situations, thus leading to more effective problem-solving and productivity.
>
> • **Collaborative Spirit**: With improved understanding and communication, teams can collaborate seamlessly, enhancing the workflow and reducing time-consuming misunderstandings.

2. Enhanced Workplace Relationships:

> •**Mutual Respect**: Recognizing and valuing the emotions of peers fosters a respectful environment. In such settings, individuals feel valued, leading to stronger workplace bonds.
>
> •**Reduced Misunderstandings**: When teams communicate with empathy and clarity, the chances of misunderstandings reduce significantly. This paves the way for a more harmonious workplace.
>
> •**Inclusivity**: Teams with high EI foster inclusivity by recognizing and respecting the diverse emotions and perspectives of all members, irrespective of their background.

3. Reduced Stress:

• Healthy Conflict Resolution: Emotionally intelligent teams address and resolve conflicts in constructive ways, preventing the buildup of stress or resentment.

• Supportive Environment: In teams where emotional well-being is valued, individuals feel more supported during challenging times, thereby reducing the feelings of isolation or overwhelm.

• Enhanced Job Satisfaction: Employees in emotionally intelligent teams often report higher job satisfaction, primarily because they feel understood, valued, and equipped to handle workplace challenges.

Imagination Infographic

Title: "The Power of Emotionally Intelligent Teamwork"

A central image of a diverse group of team members joining hands or in a collaborative pose.

Around the central image, three main segments:

1. Increased Productivity

   • Icon of a rising graph.

   • Sub-icons: Balanced scale (for decision-making) and intertwined gears (for collaboration).

2. Enhanced Workplace Relationships

   • Icon of two hands shaking.

   • Sub-icons: Heart (for mutual respect), chat bubbles (for communication), and a circle encompassing diverse faces (for inclusivity).

3. Reduced Stress

- Icon of a calm face or a relaxed individual.

- Sub-icons: Peace sign (for conflict resolution), group hug or support (for a supportive environment), and a smiley face with a checkmark (for job satisfaction).

Conclusion:

In conclusion, emotionally intelligent teamwork is not just a "nice-to-have" but a crucial element for organizations aiming for long-term success. It fosters an environment where individuals feel valued, leading to tangible benefits like productivity and intangible ones like job satisfaction. Investing in developing emotional intelligence at the team level can yield profound positive impacts for the organization as a whole.

Course 12, Section 4
Case Study
Successful Teamwork with Emotional Intelligence

Case Study: Phoenix Software & The Revival Project

Introduction:

Phoenix Software, a leading tech company, was once struggling with the development of its new AI-driven project named "Revival". With mounting pressure from stakeholders and visible cracks in the team's cohesion, they realized the project was spiraling downward. It was time to harness the power of emotional intelligence (EI) to salvage the project and the team.

The Challenge:

Revival was envisioned to be an industry game-changer. But the developmental phase was plagued with:

> 1. **Communication Gaps**: Essential information often got lost in translation. Meetings became venting sessions instead of problem-solving gatherings.

> 2. **Unresolved Conflicts**: Past disagreements became obstacles. Trust was eroding.

> 3. **Lack of Motivation**: The team was demoralized. Many were even contemplating leaving.

The Turnaround Strategy: Embracing Emotional Intelligence

To change the trajectory, the company hired Eliza, an EI coach, to facilitate the transformation.

Step 1: Emotional Awareness Sessions

Eliza began with individual sessions, letting each team member discuss their grievances, hopes, and fears. This helped in identifying the underlying emotional currents causing friction.

Step 2: Empathy Workshops

Workshops encouraged team members to step into the shoes of their colleagues. They engaged in role-reversal exercises, which proved eye-opening. The tech team better understood the pressures of marketing, while the design team gained respect for the developers' challenges.

Step 3: Constructive Feedback Mechanisms

Feedback became a tool for growth, not criticism. Eliza introduced the 'sandwich technique' – starting with a positive note, providing constructive feedback, and ending on an encouraging note.

Step 4: Group EI Activities

Group sessions involved activities promoting emotional connection, like sharing personal stories unrelated to work or team-building outdoor adventures. They also worked on shared emotional vocabulary to articulate feelings better.

Step 5: Conflict Resolution Training

Training focused on addressing the root of conflicts instead of superficial symptoms. Members learned the value of open dialogue and seeking win-win resolutions.

The Result:

Three months into the EI intervention:

1. Enhanced Communication: The team adopted 'Emotionally Charged Meetings' where members began by sharing their current emotional state. This set the tone and provided context for discussions.

2. Trust Rebuilt: Old wounds began to heal. The team became more understanding of each other's viewpoints and started trusting each other's expertise.

3. Project Progress: Revival's development accelerated. The team was now more synchronized, proactive, and solution oriented.

Conclusion

Embracing emotional intelligence didn't just rescue a project; it transformed a disjointed group of professionals into a cohesive, high-performing team. Phoenix Software's Revival became a testament not just to technological prowess but to the power of emotional connection in the workplace. The project's success and the team's renewed vigor became an inspiration throughout the company, leading to the integration of EI practices across all departments.

The Phoenix Software case underscores the transformative potential of emotional intelligence in teamwork. When challenges seem insurmountable, a focus on emotional connection, understanding, and open communication can turn the tide.

Course 12, Section 5

Practical Exercises

Teamwork and Collaboration Scenarios

Please use these exercises to check your comprehension of the material so far.

Exercise 1: The Communication Breakdown

Scenario: A team working on an innovative project is facing frequent miscommunications. Important emails are getting overlooked, meeting agendas are unclear, and tasks are being duplicated.

Task: How can you use emotional intelligence to improve communication?

Steps:

    1. Reflect: Consider a time when miscommunication affected your personal emotions and the outcome of a task. How did it feel?

    2. Empathize: Imagine being in the shoes of a team member who is consistently misunderstood. What challenges might they face?

    3. Act: Draft an email addressing the team's communication issues, applying principles of emotional intelligence.

Potential Approaches:

    1. Suggest a shared communication tool or platform.

    2. Implement weekly check-in meetings.

    3. Encourage open feedback sessions after team meetings.

Exercise 2: Navigating Team Conflicts

Scenario: Two key members of your team, Alex and Jamie, have a disagreement over the direction of a project. Their conflict is affecting the morale of the entire team.

Task: How would you mediate this conflict using emotional intelligence?

Steps:

1. **Recognize**: Identify the emotions at play. What might Alex and Jamie be feeling?

2. **Listen Actively**: Imagine a conversation with Alex and Jamie. How would you ensure you both feel heard and understood?

3. **Respond**: Design a potential solution that respects both viewpoints, aiming for a win-win outcome.

Potential Approaches:

1. Organize a mediation session.

2. Suggest a trial period for each approach, then evaluate.

3. Encourage both parties to find a middle ground or a hybrid solution.

Exercise 3: Boosting Team Morale

Scenario: After a series of project setbacks, your team's morale is low. There's visible frustration, and some members seem disengaged.

Task: How can you elevate the team's spirit and motivation using emotional intelligence?

Steps:

1. **Feel**: Remember a time when your motivation was low. What would have made you feel better?

2. **Connect**: Organize a team-building session. Consider activities that allow members to express themselves emotionally.

3. **Inspire**: Craft a motivational message, addressing the setbacks but focusing on the team's strengths and past successes.

Potential Approaches:

1. Organize a feedback and brainstorming session to address issues.

2. Host a team-building offsite day.

3. Celebrate small wins and milestones to create positive momentum.

Exercise 4: Collaborative Decision Making

Scenario: Your team has been presented with two equally compelling strategies for a project. The team is split in their preferences, leading to an impasse.

Task: How do you guide your team to a collective decision using emotional intelligence?

Steps:

1. **Understand**: Analyze the emotions behind the preferences. Are there fears, past experiences, or aspirations influencing choices?

2. **Facilitate**: Organize a decision-making workshop. Allow each side to present their strategy with emotional narratives, not just logical ones.

3. **Converge**: Use empathetic communication to understand concerns and find a blended approach or compromise.

Potential Approaches:

1. Create a pros and cons list, including emotional impacts.

2. Seek external feedback to introduce a fresh perspective.

3. Trial both strategies in smaller capacities, then analyze emotional and practical outcomes.

Conclusion

Each of these exercises immerses learners in realistic scenarios, emphasizing the importance of emotional intelligence in promoting effective teamwork and collaboration. Interactive nature allows for reflection, fostering deeper understanding and application of EI concepts.

Supplementary Material: Emotional Intelligence in Teamwork

Together We Thrive

Lucas had always prided himself on his analytical skills. As the project manager of VisionTech's leading team, he believed that numbers, timelines, and concrete results were the only things that mattered. Emotions? They were better left at home.

The team was a mix of bright minds: There was Emily, a marketing guru with an innate ability to tap into client needs; Raj, the coder who could magically bring any idea to life; Clara, a design visionary; and Noah, the strategist with a mind sharper than a blade. Each was a master of their domain, yet something was amiss.

Meetings often ended with someone upset. Emily's ideas were frequently shot down without much discussion. Raj felt unappreciated, relegated to just translating concepts into code. Clara felt stifled, her designs termed 'too out there', while Noah's strategies were often brushed aside for quicker results.

One day, after a particularly tense meeting, Lucas overheard a conversation. Emily, her voice quivering, confided in Clara, "I just don't feel like I belong here. I pour my heart into understanding our clients, but it feels like it's never enough."

That was Lucas's wake-up call. He realized that while they were a team on paper, emotionally, they were on different planets.

Enter Mrs. Aisha Green, an organizational psychologist Lucas hired to help. Aisha introduced the team to the concept of emotional intelligence, highlighting how recognizing, understanding, and managing our own emotions, and the emotions of those around us, was crucial.

The training began with self-awareness. Each team member took an emotional intelligence assessment. The results were eye-opening. Lucas was high on self-regulation but lacked empathy. Emily, on the other hand, was high on empathy but struggled with self-regulation. Each had their strengths and areas for improvement.

Next, the team was introduced to empathetic communication. Lucas learned to phrase his feedback to Emily in a more constructive manner, focusing on how she might feel. Emily, in turn, learned to express her frustrations without letting them cloud her judgment.

Clara and Noah engaged in a role-playing session. Clara, playing the part of Noah, had to defend a strategy she didn't believe in. This exercise fostered mutual respect and understanding. They grasped the significance of perspective-taking.

Raj's transformation was the most visible. He was encouraged to share more about his process, making the rest of the team realize the complexity and genius behind what he did. They began to see the emotion behind the code.

As weeks turned into months, the VisionTech team was hardly recognizable. Meetings were collaborative spaces where ideas flowed freely. Emotions weren't suppressed; they were harnessed.

One day, faced with a challenging project pivot, Lucas suggested, "Why don't we all take a moment to consider how this change might affect each of us emotionally? Understanding that might guide our strategy."

The project was a resounding success, not just in terms of output but the harmony with which it was executed.

VisionTech's top brass noticed. They inquired, "Lucas, what changed? Your team's dynamics seem... different."

Lucas smiled, "We learned that numbers and deadlines have their place. But to truly excel, we needed to embrace the emotions, ours and others. That's the true essence of teamwork."

From then on, VisionTech's mantra was clear: Logic drives processes, but emotional intelligence drives people. And its people who drive success.

Parting Thoughts

As with previous courses, be sure to include regular pauses for reflection and personal application throughout the course to ensure learners can relate the content back to their own workplace experiences.

Course 13
Emotional Intelligence in the Workplace
Part 2
Leadership and Influence

Learning Objectives for Course 13

1. Understand the role of emotional intelligence in effective leadership and influence.

2. Learn how to leverage emotional intelligence to build influence in the workplace.

3. Develop strategies for leading with emotional intelligence.

Course 13, Section 1
Introduction to Leadership and Emotional Intelligence

The Interconnected Web of Leadership and Emotional Intelligence (EI)

At its core, leadership is about influencing and guiding others towards a common goal or vision. To be effective in this role, a leader must be attuned not just to strategic metrics or performance benchmarks, but to the pulse of the people they lead. This is where emotional intelligence comes into play.

Emotional intelligence refers to an individual's capacity to recognize, understand, manage, and effectively use emotions — both their own and those of others. In the realm of leadership, emotional intelligence becomes a cornerstone for numerous reasons:

>   1. **Understanding Motivations**: Leaders with high EI can delve deeper into what drives their team members, fostering a workplace where employees feel understood and valued.

>   2. **Enhancing Communication**: Emotionally intelligent leaders listen with empathy, allowing for open and constructive communication channels.

>   3. **Managing Conflict**: Leader's adept in EI can foresee potential conflicts and navigate through them smoothly, ensuring team harmony and productivity.

>   4. **Building Trust**: Recognizing and valuing the emotions of team members builds a foundation of trust, crucial for any leadership role.

Key Leadership Competencies Influenced by Emotional Intelligence:

>   1. **Self-awareness**: Recognizing one's emotions and their effects. Leaders who exhibit this are in tune with their strengths and weaknesses and can lead with authenticity.

2. **Self-regulation**: The ability to control disruptive emotions and impulses. Leaders skilled in this competency display patience, remain calm under pressure, and are adaptable to change.

3. **Motivation**: Being driven to achieve beyond expectations, stemming from internal passion rather than external factors. Motivated leaders have a clear vision and show enthusiasm towards their goals.

4. **Empathy**: Understanding and sharing the feelings of another. Empathetic leaders consider the emotions of their team members, allowing for better rapport and team cohesion.

5. **Social skills**: Building and managing relationships to move people in the desired direction. Leaders with good social skills are adept at building networks, fostering collaboration, and promoting team harmony.

Conclusion:

In conclusion, leadership, while a multifaceted role, becomes significantly more effective with the integration of emotional intelligence. An emotionally intelligent leader doesn't just lead a team; they inspire, understand, and elevate every individual, ensuring that the journey towards the goal is as enriching as the achievement itself.

Course 13, Section 2
Emotional Intelligence and Influence

Emotional intelligence (EI) is not merely a set of soft skills or a professional buzzword. It is a transformative tool in the realm of leadership and influence. Influence is not about wielding power but about impacting perspectives, behaviors, and attitudes. A leader's capability to influence is intertwined with their ability to connect, understand, and resonate with others, which is precisely where EI shines.

Let's delve into the pivotal ways emotional intelligence plays a role in building genuine influence:

1. **Recognizing and Understanding Others' Emotions**:

   • **Contextual Understanding**: By detecting and deciphering the emotions of others, leaders can gauge the pulse of their team or audience. This awareness allows for a tailored approach to communication, ensuring that messages are both relevant and resonant.

   • **Predictive Insight**: Recognizing patterns in emotional responses provides leaders with the foresight to anticipate reactions, enabling them to address concerns proactively rather than reactively.

2. **Demonstrating Empathy**:

   • **Building Trust**: Empathy goes beyond mere understanding; it's about valuing and validating others' experiences. Leaders who genuinely empathize build a foundation of trust, essential for influence.

   • **Boosting Morale and Loyalty**: When team members or stakeholders feel understood and valued, it fosters a sense of loyalty and belonging. They are more likely to be aligned with a leader's vision when they believe the leader genuinely cares about their well-being.

- **Facilitating Open Communication**: An empathetic environment promotes open dialogue. People are more inclined to share ideas, feedback, and concerns when they believe they'll be heard and understood.

3. **Managing One's Emotions Effectively**:

    - **Leading by Example**: Leaders who exhibit emotional stability set the tone for the entire team or organization. When leaders respond to challenges with calm and clarity, it encourages similar behavior throughout.

    - **Enhanced Decision Making**: By managing emotions, leaders can ensure their decisions are based on a balanced blend of emotion and logic, leading to more informed and holistic choices.

    - **Maintaining Influence During Crisis**: Crisis situations can be a real test of a leader's influence. Those with high EI maintain their composure, ensuring their influence remains intact even during tumultuous times.

4. **Leveraging Emotional Appeals in Arguments**:

    - **Connecting on a Deeper Level**: Facts and logic are crucial, but to truly influence, one must connect emotionally. Emotionally intelligent leaders know how to weave emotional appeals into their arguments, making them more compelling.

Conclusion:

In conclusion, the potency of influence is not solely based on the strength of arguments or the hierarchy of positions. It's derived from a leader's capacity to connect, empathize, and resonate. Through emotional intelligence, leaders can cultivate an influence that is both profound and lasting, creating ripples of positive impact throughout their sphere of operation.

Course 13, Section 3

Strategies for Leading with Emotional Intelligence

1. Self-awareness

Definition: Self-awareness involves understanding one's emotions, triggers, strengths, and weaknesses, allowing for introspection and growth.

Role-play Scenario: "The Overbooked Schedule"

Scene: The office of Caroline, a department head, is filled with her team members. They're discussing multiple projects, and Caroline realizes she's overcommitted herself.

Caroline (feeling the stress mounting): "I've taken on so many projects that I'm not sure how I'll manage to give each the attention it deserves."

Mark (concerned): "We have noticed that you've been juggling a lot lately, Caroline."

Caroline (pausing to reflect): "You're right, Mark. I appreciate your concern. I've realized my tendency to overcommit, and I need to address this. Let's prioritize these projects and see how we can delegate or reschedule some."

Sophie: "We're here to help, Caroline. Let's figure it out together."

Discussion: Caroline's self-awareness allowed her to recognize her emotions and the impact of her decisions. By admitting her oversight and actively seeking solutions, she not only found a way forward but also strengthened her team's trust in her leadership.

2. Emotional Regulation

Definition: Emotional regulation is the ability to control one's emotions, ensuring reactions are constructive, especially in challenging situations.

Role-play Scenario: "The Failed Project"

Scene: A conference room where Michael, the CEO, is addressing a team that just had a project fail.

Michael (feeling disappointed but taking a deep breath): "It's clear that the project didn't go as planned. But pointing fingers isn't going to help. Let's discuss what went wrong and how we can learn from it."

Anna (looking down): "I'm sorry, Michael. I know I played a part in the miscommunication."

Michael (calmly): "Anna, this isn't about blame. We're a team. Let's focus on the lessons learned and how we can improve our processes."

Discussion: Michael's ability to regulate his emotions ensured a constructive conversation. Instead of fostering a culture of blame, he emphasized learning and growth, reinforcing a positive and supportive work environment.

3. Empathetic Communication

Definition: This strategy is about understanding and sharing another's feelings, facilitating open communication that's sensitive to the emotional state of others.

Role-play Scenario: "Burnout Beckons"

Scene: An office where Emma, a team leader, is speaking to Ryan, a team member who's been putting in many late nights.

Emma (noticing dark circles under Ryan's eyes): "Ryan, I've seen you working late quite often. How are you holding up?"

Ryan (sighing): "It's been tough, Emma. I'm trying to meet the deadlines, but I feel like I'm on the verge of burning out."

Emma (compassionately): "Your well-being is important. Let's discuss how we can manage the workload or get additional resources. Remember, it's okay to ask for help."

Discussion: Emma's empathetic approach allowed Ryan to open up about his struggles. By acknowledging and addressing his feelings, she showcased a leadership style that values the well-being of her team members, leading to increased trust and loyalty.

Conclusion

Each of these role-play scenarios underscores the importance of integrating emotional intelligence into leadership. When leaders demonstrate self-awareness, emotional regulation, and empathetic communication, they foster a positive workplace culture, emphasizing collaboration, understanding, and mutual respect.

Course 13, Section 4

Case Study – Leading with Emotional Intelligence

The Transformation of Atlas Corp:
The Journey of CEO Eleanor Reed

Introduction

Atlas Corp, a once-thriving software company, had hit hard times. Innovation had slowed, employee morale was at an all-time low, and profits were plummeting. When Eleanor Reed took over as CEO, she knew she had to do more than just streamline processes and cut costs.

The Challenge

Eleanor's first town hall meeting was an eye-opener. Employees voiced concerns about feeling undervalued, overworked, and disconnected from the company's vision. There was a clear lack of trust between the management and employees. High employee turnover rates and internal conflicts have become commonplace.

Eleanor's Approach

1. **Self-awareness**:

In her initial days, Eleanor took time to introspect. She recognized her apprehension about taking on a company in turmoil but also realized her genuine concern for its people. Admitting her anxieties to her leadership team, she initiated open discussions about their collective strengths and weaknesses.

2. **Emotional Regulation**:

In one instance, a product launch faced a massive setback due to a technical glitch. Instead of placing blame, Eleanor called for a meeting. She started by acknowledging the disappointment and then steered the conversation towards understanding the root cause and ensuring such mistakes wouldn't be repeated.

3. **Empathetic Communication**:

Eleanor set up monthly one-on-one meetings with team leads and regular open forums where employees could voice concerns. She made an effort to genuinely listen and understand the underlying emotions behind their words.

The Turning Point

About six months into her tenure, Atlas Corp faced a potential PR disaster. A dissatisfied client aired grievances on social media. The news went viral. Eleanor convened an emergency meeting.

Instead of panicking, she employed the emotional intelligence techniques she'd been cultivating:

- She began by openly discussing her feelings of concern about the company's reputation, evoking a sense of collective responsibility.

- She empathetically acknowledged the stress the PR crisis was causing the team, especially the communications department.

- She ensured the conversation didn't devolve into a blame game, focusing instead on proactive solutions.

The team decided to openly acknowledge the oversight, apologize to the client publicly, and lay out steps to ensure it wouldn't happen again. The transparent approach was well-received, turning potential negative publicity into an example of accountability.

The Outcomes

Over the next year, Atlas Corp experienced:

- A 40% reduction in employee turnover.

- A 20% increase in productivity.

- A noticeable improvement in workplace morale and employee satisfaction scores.

- A revived innovation drive, resulting in two successful product launches.

Discussion Questions

1. How did Eleanor's emotional intelligence strategies play a role in turning around Atlas Corp's fortunes?

Answer: Eleanor's application of emotional intelligence strategies, including self-awareness, emotional regulation, and empathetic communication, fostered an environment of trust, transparency, and open dialogue. This shifted the organizational culture from one of blame and mistrust to one of collaboration and collective responsibility.

2. In the PR crisis, how did Eleanor's approach contrast with how such crises are typically handled?

Answer: Often, organizations respond defensively to PR crises, attempting to shift blame or downplay the issue. Eleanor, leveraging her emotional intelligence, chose transparency, accountability, and proactive solutions. This not only resolved the immediate crisis but also enhanced the company's reputation.

3. How can leaders ensure that their self-awareness doesn't come across as self-centeredness?

Answer: True self-awareness is balanced with an understanding and appreciation for others' perspectives and feelings. Leaders, while being aware of their emotions and strengths, should also be attuned to the emotions of their team, demonstrating genuine concern and understanding.

Conclusion

Eleanor Reed's journey with Atlas Corp underscores the transformative power of emotional intelligence in leadership. By prioritizing emotional connections and understanding, she was able to revitalize a floundering company and inspire a new era of success and innovation.

Course 13, Section 5

Practical Exercises: 3 Leadership Scenarios for Practice

1. Role Play: Using Self-awareness in Leadership Decisions

Scenario: You're the new manager at Innovative, and you've been asked to spearhead an important project that would determine the company's direction for the next five years. You feel immense pressure to perform but are also nervous about leading such a crucial endeavor.

Role Play:

Choice A: You suppress your anxieties and try to project an overly confident demeanor, claiming you have everything under control, even when team members ask if they can assist in any way.

Choice B: In your team meeting, you admit you're feeling the weight of this responsibility and ask for everyone's active collaboration and feedback throughout the process.

Choice C: You decide not to tell anyone about your anxieties and instead delegate most of your duties to a senior team member.

Discussion:

• **Choice A** might make you appear confident initially but could alienate team members who sense a lack of genuineness and may feel undervalued.

• **Choice B** leverages self-awareness to foster trust, inclusivity, and team cohesion. It displays vulnerability, which, when used appropriately, can be a strength in leadership.

• **Choice C** avoids the issue entirely, which can lead to feelings of mistrust and speculation among the team.

Best Choice: Choice B. By being self-aware and transparent about your feelings, you encourage open communication and a collaborative environment.

2. Role Play: Emotional Intelligence and Influence

Scenario: Your department has been asked to work overtime to complete a project, leading to widespread dissatisfaction. As a leader, you need to influence your team to see the larger picture without dismissing their emotions.

Role Play:

Choice A: You give a directive statement: "Overtime is mandatory. The company relies on us."

Choice B: Arrange a team meeting where you express your understanding of their feelings, explain the company's position, and ask for their support.

Choice C: Offer incentives like bonuses or extra days off without addressing the underlying discontent.

Discussion:

- **Choice A** lacks empathy and may lead to further resentment and reduced morale.
- **Choice B** shows empathy and understanding, offers clarity, and makes the team feel valued.
- **Choice C** provides a temporary solution but does not address the root of the dissatisfaction.

Best Choice: Choice B. Using emotional intelligence to validate their feelings and provide context can influence the team positively.

3. Role Play: Leading with Empathetic Communication

Scenario: A member of your team, Alex, has been underperforming recently. You've learned that Alex is going through a divorce.

Role Play:

Choice A: Ignore Alex's personal issues and reprimand him for the dip in performance.

Choice B: Schedule a private meeting with Alex to understand his situation and discuss potential solutions.

Choice C: Publicly acknowledge Alex's situation in a team meeting and assure him that the team supports him.

Discussion:

- **Choice A** lacks empathy and understanding, potentially leading to further performance issues and resentment.

- **Choice B** uses empathetic communication to address the issue privately, showing concern while also addressing the performance dip.

- **Choice C**, while well-intentioned, might embarrass Alex and expose his private issues unnecessarily.

Best Choice: Choice B. Addressing the issue privately with empathy and understanding respects Alex's privacy and maintains professional boundaries.

Conclusion:

These role plays provide insights into how the principles of emotional intelligence can be applied in real-world leadership scenarios. By considering the implications of each choice, learners can better understand the importance and application of emotional intelligence in leadership.

Supplementary Material: Emotional Intelligence in Leadership

Leaders of Influence

Clara Burns ascended to the role of CEO at Dynamic Tech, a leading tech conglomerate. The previous CEO had been a man of immense technical know-how, but his leadership style was more autocratic than democratic, creating subtle rifts in the organization. Employees whispered in the coffee nooks about missed opportunities, feeling unheard, and their mounting stress. As Clara took the helm, she recognized these undercurrents. Having risen from the ranks, she knew she couldn't lead with just business acumen; emotional intelligence was the call of the hour.

On her first day, instead of sending out a generic email or making a broad announcement, Clara opted for a series of town-hall meetings, providing a platform for open dialogue. Demonstrating her self-awareness, she began by expressing her feelings. "I'm honored but also daunted by the responsibility. I want this company to thrive, not just in terms of revenue, but as a community."

Her candidness was met with appreciation. Employees felt an immediate difference. Here was a CEO who wasn't just talking to them but with them.

As weeks turned into months, Clara recognized a brewing issue with Project Orion, one of the firm's flagship initiatives. Timelines were slipping, and the team seemed despondent. Instead of summoning the team leads for an explanation, Clara decided to sit in on one of their brainstorming sessions. It was here she noticed Mark, a usually enthusiastic team member, looking withdrawn.

Utilizing her empathetic communication skills, she invited Mark for a coffee chat. Mark hesitated initially but eventually shared his concerns about some technical aspects of the project, fearing backlash for dissent. Clara thanked him for his honesty and assured him that every viewpoint, especially those that challenge the status quo, were vital.

The word spread. Clara wasn't just a figurehead; she was actively shaping a culture where employees felt valued and heard. She emphasized the importance of understanding others' emotions as leaders, empowering managers with training to be more attuned to their team's emotional well-being.

One afternoon, as she reviewed quarterly numbers, Clara's personal assistant, Lydia, rushed in, distress evident in her eyes. Her mother was unwell, and she felt torn between her responsibilities. Demonstrating emotional regulation, Clara calmly suggested, "Lydia, family comes first. We'll manage here. Take the time you need." The ripple effect of this single act of kindness fortified the sentiment that Dynamic Tech was transforming under Clara's emotionally intelligent leadership.

However, the true test came during the annual stakeholder meeting. A significant product failure had caused stocks to dip, and disgruntled shareholders demanded answers. Clara, leveraging her influence and understanding of emotions, calmly acknowledged their concerns. She shared the corrective steps in place, but also highlighted success stories, weaving in testimonials from employees about the positive shift in company culture.

Post the meeting, a senior stakeholder, Mrs. Fernandez, remarked, "I've been a part of these meetings for a decade. Today, I saw a leader truly connected with her company, not just its balance sheets."

Clara's influence was not limited to managing crises. She began mentorship programs, pairing senior leaders with newer employees, focusing not just on job roles but emotional growth. Managers were encouraged to practice self-awareness and empathetic communication, leading to teams feeling more cohesive and understood.

Under Clara's leadership, Dynamic Tech didn't just recover its stock prices but also became a beacon for emotionally intelligent leadership. Employee turnover reduced, job satisfaction scores soared, and the company started attracting top talent, not just for its market position but its positive work culture.

As years passed, Clara's legacy was not just the profits she garnered but the leaders she nurtured. Leaders who knew that numbers mattered, but it was the people behind those numbers that made all the difference.

And so, at Dynamic Tech, the story was told and retold – of Clara Burns, a leader of influence, a beacon of emotional intelligence.

Discussion:

This story underscores the pivotal role emotional intelligence plays in leadership. Clara's actions, from understanding employee sentiments to addressing stakeholder concerns, highlight the core principles discussed in Lesson 13. As you reflect on the story, consider how emotional intelligence can become your leadership superpower, transforming not just businesses, but lives.

Parting Thoughts

As with the previous courses, be sure to include regular pauses for reflection and personal application, so learners can relate the content back to their own leadership experiences or aspirations.

Course 14
Emotional Intelligence in the Workplace
Part 3
Managing Stress and Burnout

Learning Objectives for Course 14

1. Understand the role of emotional intelligence in managing workplace stress and preventing burnout.

2. Learn strategies to manage stress and prevent burnout using emotional intelligence.

3. Apply emotional intelligence skills in practical scenarios to manage stress and prevent burnout.

Course 14, Section 1

Introduction to Stress, Burnout, and Emotional Intelligence

Stress and burnout have become ubiquitous terms in the modern workplace. With increasing demands, longer hours, and the blurring lines between personal and professional lives, especially in a digital era, more individuals are feeling the weight of these challenges.

Stress is a natural physical and mental reaction to life experiences. Short-term, it can be beneficial by helping you avoid danger or meet a deadline. However, long-term, chronic stress can lead to severe health problems and negatively impact job performance and satisfaction.

Burnout, on the other hand, is a state of emotional, physical, and mental exhaustion caused by prolonged stress. It's characterized by feelings of cynicism, detachment from one's job, and a sense of ineffectiveness.

This is where emotional intelligence comes into play. With a keen awareness of our own emotions and those of others, as well as the skills to manage these emotions, individuals can more effectively cope with stressors, reduce the risk of burnout, and foster a more positive work environment.

Imagination Infographic

Title: The Triad of Emotional Wellness in the Workplace

1. Stress

> **Image**: A clock with racing hands, a pile of papers, and a computer with multiple notifications popping up.
>
> **Description**: The body's reaction to challenging situations, both positive and negative.

2. **Burnout**

> **Image**: A candle burning at both ends, with a worker looking exhausted in the background, hands on their head.
>
> **Description**: Emotional and physical exhaustion from prolonged stress.

3. **Emotional Intelligence (EI)**

> **Image**: A brain with glowing areas signifying awareness and a heart interconnected, showing empathy and understanding.
>
> **Description**: The ability to recognize, understand, and manage our own emotions, as well as to recognize, understand, and influence the emotions of others.

At the bottom of the infographic: With EI, Navigate Stress & Prevent Burnout.

Conclusion

Understanding the dynamics of stress, burnout, and emotional intelligence allows employees and leaders alike to address challenges proactively, ensuring not only a more productive workplace but also a happier and more fulfilled workforce. Recognizing the symptoms and employing emotionally intelligent strategies can make the difference between floundering in a challenging environment and flourishing despite it.

Course 14, Section 2
Recognizing Stress and Burnout

Stress and burnout, although often used interchangeably, are distinct experiences. Stress is characterized by over-engagement, hyperactivity, and anxiety, whereas burnout is about disengagement, emotional blunting, and detachment.

Signs of Stress Include:

- Physical symptoms like headaches, muscle tension, and chest pain.
- Emotional symptoms such as irritability, anxiety, and mood swings.
- Behavioral changes like changes in appetite or sleep patterns.

Signs of Burnout Include:

- Feeling emotionally drained and unable to cope.
- Detachment from work or becoming cynical about work.
- Reduced professional efficacy or a feeling of not achieving anything meaningful.

Case Study 1: Sarah's Overwhelming Stress

Sarah had always been the go-to person in her marketing department, known for her dedication and willingness to work late. When the company decided to launch a new product, Sarah was naturally entrusted with the lead role in marketing. However, alongside her existing duties, the added responsibility began to take its toll. Sarah would often wake up in the middle of the night, heart racing, thinking about work. She'd snap at colleagues over minor issues and started relying on junk food and caffeine to get through the day. Her usually impeccable work began showing errors, and she was perpetually tired.

One day, a colleague found Sarah in tears in the break room. Concerned, the colleague urged Sarah to talk to her manager. When she did, Sarah realized she was showing classic signs of workplace stress. Her manager suggested a temporary assistant and a few days off to recharge.

Discussion: Sarah's experience underscores the importance of balance. While dedication to one's job is commendable, it shouldn't come at the cost of personal well-being. Recognizing signs of stress early on and seeking intervention is key to ensuring it doesn't escalate to burnout. The proactive approach of Sarah's colleague and manager helped Sarah recalibrate and approach her work in a healthier way.

Case Study 2: Daniel's Slow Descent into Burnout

Daniel was a seasoned software engineer, always passionate about coding and solving complex problems. Over the years, however, he noticed that his enthusiasm was waning. He began to dread Mondays, became increasingly impatient with his team, and felt that his efforts made little difference. Projects he would once tackle with gusto now seemed meaningless. Feedback sessions left him feeling indifferent, and he started isolating himself.

It was during a team-building workshop that a segment on burnout resonated with Daniel. Realizing he might be going through it, he approached the HR department, which connected him with a counselor. Through counseling, Daniel realized that he had lost sight of his professional and personal goals and felt disconnected from his purpose. He then took a sabbatical, traveled, attended tech conferences, and returned to work with a renewed passion.

Discussion: Burnout isn't always about excessive workload; it can also stem from a lack of purpose or connection to the job. Daniel's story is a reminder that even seasoned professionals can experience burnout, and it's essential to reconnect with one's purpose and passion. By recognizing the signs and seeking help, professionals can rediscover their love for their vocation.

Conclusion: Recognizing the signs of stress and burnout is the first step towards addressing them. It's essential to remember that everyone, irrespective of their profession or seniority, can experience these feelings. Taking a proactive approach, seeking support, and understanding one's limits can ensure a healthier relationship with one's work.

Course 14, Section 3

Emotional Intelligence Techniques for Managing Stress

Emotional Intelligence Techniques for Managing Stress

Emotional intelligence (EI) is not just about understanding and managing emotions in interpersonal relationships. It's also crucial for self-management, especially when facing stress. By harnessing the power of emotional intelligence, individuals can better handle stressors and enhance their overall well-being. Here are some core emotional intelligence techniques to manage stress:

1. **Self-awareness**:

Definition: Self-awareness is the ability to recognize and understand one's own emotions as they occur. This awareness is fundamental in recognizing the onset of stress.

Application:

- **Journaling**: Regularly writing down feelings can help in identifying patterns or specific triggers that cause stress.

- **Mindful Meditation**: Taking a few minutes each day to meditate can help in gaining awareness of one's emotional state.

2. **Emotional Regulation**:

Definition: Emotional regulation refers to the ability to manage and respond to an emotional experience in a controlled manner.

Application:

- **Reframing**: Change the narrative of the situation. Instead of thinking, "I'll never get this done," consider, "I will prioritize tasks and handle them one by one."

- **Breathing Exercises**: During high-stress moments, deep, controlled breathing can calm the mind and provide clarity.

- **Timeout**: Sometimes, stepping away from a stressful situation, even if just for a few minutes, can help in regaining emotional control.

3. **Self-care Strategies**:

Definition: Self-care involves activities and practices we engage in on a regular basis to reduce stress and maintain our well-being.

Application:

- **Physical Activity**: Regular exercise, even a short walk, can release endorphins, natural stress relievers.

- **Healthy Eating**: Consuming a balanced diet ensures that the body and brain have the necessary nutrients to function optimally.

- **Sleep**: Adequate rest is crucial. Establishing a regular sleep schedule and ensuring the sleep environment is conducive can make a huge difference in stress levels.

- **Hobbies and Interests**: Engaging in activities outside of work, be it reading, painting, or any other hobby, can serve as an excellent mental escape and stress reducer.

4. **Empathy for Self**:

Definition: Often overlooked, self-empathy is the compassion we show to ourselves. It's recognizing that it's okay to ask for help or take a break.

Application:

- **Positive Self-talk**: Instead of being critical, use encouraging language with oneself.

- **Seeking Support**: Whether it's professional counseling or simply talking to a friend, acknowledging the need for help is crucial.

5. **Limit Setting**:

Definition: Knowing when to say "no" or set boundaries to avoid overextending oneself.

Application:

- Prioritizing Tasks: Recognize what's essential and what can wait.
- Delegate: If possible, share responsibilities with others.

Conclusion

Stress, when left unchecked, can lead to burnout and other severe health conditions. Leveraging emotional intelligence techniques not only helps in managing stress but also in building resilience against future stressors. By cultivating these skills, one can navigate life's challenges more effectively and maintain a healthy balance between work and personal well-being.

Course 14, Section 4
Emotional Intelligence Strategies to Prevent Burnout

Burnout, a state of emotional, physical, and mental exhaustion caused by prolonged and excessive stress, has detrimental effects on one's well-being and performance. When individuals reach burnout, they often feel drained, unable to meet continuous demands, and eventually lose interest and motivation. Emotional intelligence (EI) can play a pivotal role in preventing burnout by equipping individuals with tools and strategies to handle stress proactively. Let's delve into these strategies:

1. **Maintaining Work-Life Balance**:

Definition: Achieving a balance between professional demands and personal life ensures overall well-being and reduces the chances of burnout.

EI Application:

- **Self-awareness**: Recognize when you're tipping the scale too much towards work and neglecting personal or family time.

- **Self-regulation**: Discipline yourself to disconnect from work, especially during personal time or vacations.

2. **Setting Boundaries**:

Definition: Clearly defining what is acceptable and what isn't in terms of work hours, availability, and task delegation.

EI Application:

- **Assertiveness**: Use your EI skills to communicate your needs and set limits without coming across as aggressive.

- **Self-awareness**: Recognize when you're stretching yourself too thin and when to say no.

3. **Practicing Empathy**:

Definition: The ability to understand and share the feelings of another.

EI Application:

- Understanding Team Members: Recognizing signs of stress or discomfort in colleagues can lead to collaborative solutions to decrease workload or provide support.

- Enhancing Interpersonal Relationships: Building strong, empathetic relationships at work can serve as a support system during demanding times.

4. **Self-compassion and Understanding**:

Definition: Treating oneself with the same kindness and understanding as one would treat a friend.

EI Application:

- Positive Self-talk: Being aware of negative self-criticism and intentionally reframing such thoughts.

- Acknowledging Limitations: Recognizing that it's human to have limitations and that it's okay to ask for help or take breaks when needed.

5. **Regular Self-assessment**:

Definition: Regularly evaluating one's emotional health and well-being.

EI Application:

- Emotional Awareness: Periodically checking in with oneself to gauge stress levels and emotional state.

- Seeking Feedback: Occasionally seeking feedback from peers or supervisors to ensure that one's perception matches the reality of their performance.

6. Professional Development and Learning:

Definition: Continuously updating one's skills and knowledge.

EI Application:

> • Growth Mindset: Cultivating a mindset where challenges are seen as opportunities for growth rather than threats.
>
> • Seeking Mentoring: Finding a mentor can provide guidance, emotional support, and perspective.

Conclusion

Burnout isn't merely about being tired or overworked; it's about feeling unsupported, unappreciated, and trapped. Emotional intelligence provides a robust framework to recognize the onset of burnout symptoms and actively counteract them. By integrating these EI-based strategies, one can create a sustainable work environment, ensuring long-term success and well-being.

Course 14, Section 5

Practical Exercises: Stress Management Scenarios

Exercise 1: Balancing Work and Life

Scenario: Jane is a software developer who's been working late hours for weeks on a project. She feels the burnout creeping in, especially as her young son misses spending evenings with her.

Role-play Script:

Manager: Jane, I noticed you've been staying late often. How's the project going?

Jane: It's progressing, but it's taking more time than I anticipated. I've been feeling stressed, and my son misses me at home.

Manager: I appreciate your dedication. Maybe we can look at delegating some tasks or getting you some assistance? It's essential for you to balance work and personal life.

Summary Discussion: This scenario highlights the importance of self-awareness in recognizing burnout symptoms and the value of assertive communication to set boundaries. Managers practicing empathy can make a significant difference in reducing the stress of their team members.

Exercise 2: Setting Personal Boundaries

Scenario: Ravi often gets emails late at night from his colleague, Mike, expecting immediate responses. This disrupts Ravi's family time.

Role-play Script:

Ravi: Mike, I've noticed I get many emails from you late in the evening. While I understand the urgency, it's challenging to respond immediately as I'm usually spending time with my family then.

Mike: Oh, I didn't realize it was an issue. I just thought I'd send them as I work on them.

Ravi: I understand. Can we set a specific time frame during which we handle work-related communications? It'll help me manage my time better.

Summary Discussion: This interaction underscores the importance of being self-aware and assertively communicating personal boundaries, ensuring both work efficiency and personal well-being.

Exercise 3: Empathy towards Overwhelmed Colleague

Scenario: Carla observes her colleague, Ahmed, looking visibly stressed, juggling multiple tasks simultaneously.

Role-play Script:

Carla: Ahmed, you seem a bit overwhelmed. Want to talk about it?

Ahmed: Thanks, Carla. Yes, I've just been assigned two new projects, and I'm finding it hard to manage everything.

Carla: I've been there. Let me know if you need help prioritizing or if I can assist in any other way. Remember, it's okay to ask for support.

Summary Discussion: The exercise showcases the power of empathy in recognizing signs of stress in others and offering support, which can greatly alleviate feelings of being overwhelmed.

Exercise 4: Self-compassion in Mistakes

Scenario: Alex made an error in a client presentation. Instead of berating himself, he practices self-compassion.

Role-play Script:

Alex (thinking): I can't believe I made that mistake in the presentation. But everyone makes mistakes. I'll correct it and ensure it doesn't happen next time.

Colleague: Alex, I noticed the error. Are you okay?

Alex: Thanks for checking in. Yes, I realized it too. I'll be more vigilant next time. I've learned from this.

Summary Discussion: This scenario emphasizes the significance of self-compassion. By recognizing mistakes without excessive self-criticism, individuals can grow from experiences, leading to resilience against stress.

Exercise 5: Prioritizing Self-care

Scenario: Lisa feels exhausted, missing out on her yoga classes due to extended work hours.

Role-play Script:

Lisa's friend: Hey, haven't seen you at yoga recently. Everything okay?

Lisa: Work has been crazy, and I've been skipping yoga to catch up.

Lisa's friend: Remember, taking time for yourself helps you recharge. Maybe adjust your schedule? Yoga helps you handle stress better.

Lisa: You're right. I need to prioritize self-care. I'll start by attending tomorrow's class.

Summary Discussion: The exercise underscores the essence of self-awareness in recognizing the need for self-care and its role in preventing burnout and managing stress effectively.

Supplementary Material: Emotional Intelligence, Stress, and Burnout

Balancing Act

Renee was the epitome of success in her marketing firm. Known for her dedication and resilience, she was often the first to arrive and the last to leave. The panoramic view from her glass-walled office showed a city that never slept, much like her.

One evening, as the city lights twinkled, her colleague, Jackson, knocked on her door. "Another late night?" he asked, raising an eyebrow.

She sighed. "This campaign is crucial. The stakes are high."

Jackson, sensing the strain in her voice, gently probed, "Renee, when was the last time you took a day off?"

She laughed, "Who has the time?"

The weeks that followed saw Renee pushing herself harder. Sleep was scarce, meals were often forgotten, and yoga - which once was her solace - became a distant memory. She began to notice signs of fatigue but brushed them off, attributing them to the 'busy phase.'

On a fateful Wednesday, during a presentation with a critical client, Renee's exhaustion caught up with her. She mixed up the figures, leading to a confused narrative. The room was filled with awkward silences and exchanged glances.

Post the meeting, her boss, Mr. Thompson, called her in. Expecting a reprimand, Renee braced herself. Instead, she found empathy.

"I've noticed you're burning the candle at both ends," he began. "Your dedication is commendable, but today's mishap was avoidable. It's evident you're stressed, maybe even on the verge of burnout."

She looked down, "I thought I could handle it."

Mr. Thompson, pausing for a moment, responded, "Emotional intelligence isn't just about understanding others but understanding ourselves. Recognizing when we're overwhelmed and taking steps to manage it."

Over the next few weeks, with Mr. Thompson's encouragement, Renee began attending a program on Emotional Intelligence at work. She learned about recognizing signs of stress and burnout. As she listened to others share, she realized how her lack of self-awareness had put her work and health at risk.

Renee decided to re-introduce yoga into her life, ensuring she attended sessions thrice a week. The sense of calm and clarity she felt after each class was undeniable.

Additionally, she started setting boundaries. No work-related emails or calls after 7 PM. Weekends were strictly for rejuvenation - reading, hiking, spending time with loved ones, or just catching up on sleep.

At work, Renee initiated regular check-ins with her team, creating an environment where everyone felt safe to express their feelings and concerns. This not only led to a healthier work atmosphere but also more innovative and creative ideas.

One day, as she sat enjoying a cup of tea, Jackson walked in, "The new campaign strategy your team presented was brilliant!"

Renee smiled, "It's a team effort. By ensuring everyone's well-being, we can think more clearly and work more effectively."

Jackson nodded in agreement, "You seem different, more... balanced."

Renee took a deep breath, the kind that reaches your soul, "I've learned that success isn't about running a never-ending race. It's about pacing yourself, understanding your emotions, and most importantly, ensuring you're not just physically but also emotionally present in everything you do."

As days turned into weeks and weeks into months, the marketing firm saw a positive shift. Productivity was up, and absenteeism was down. Renee's transformation had a ripple effect.

Renee's journey was a testament to the power of emotional intelligence in recognizing, addressing, and preventing stress and burnout. Her story served as a beacon, illuminating the path for many in the corporate maze, reminding them of the delicate yet crucial balancing act.

Renee's story embodies the essence of lesson 14. It's about recognizing when one's tipping into the realms of unhealthy stress and potential burnout and using emotional intelligence to navigate back to a balanced state. The story underscores that true success isn't just about relentless hard work but also about emotional well-being and self-awareness.

Parting Thoughts

As with the previous courses, encourage learners to reflect and apply the learned strategies in their own life. These real-world applications and personal experiences are critical in embedding the learning for long-term benefit.

Course 15
Developing Your Emotional Intelligence Practice and Growth

Learning Objectives for Course 15

1. Understand the importance of ongoing practice and growth in emotional intelligence.

2. Learn about strategies and exercises that support the continued development of emotional intelligence.

3. Apply emotional intelligence strategies and exercises in daily life.

Course 15, Section 1

The Journey of Emotional Intelligence

Introduction

Emotional Intelligence (EI) is not a destination, but a journey. It's an evolving skillset that requires consistent nurturing, refinement, and application. Unlike a static trait, EI can be cultivated and developed over time, making it a dynamic facet of personal and professional growth. Just as athletes continually train to maintain and enhance their physical prowess, individuals must also consistently practice emotional intelligence to reap its full benefits.

The Ongoing Nature of Emotional Intelligence Development

1. **Continuous Learning**: Emotional landscapes change as we encounter different life stages, challenges, and experiences. Hence, our understanding and handling of emotions need to adapt accordingly. What works in one's twenties may need re-evaluation in their forties.

2. **Adaptability**: The world is in constant flux. Societal norms, professional demands, relationships, and personal circumstances change, demanding our emotional adaptability. Stagnation in emotional skills can lead to decreased resilience and flexibility in the face of change.

3. **Deepening Understanding**: Early in one's EI journey, understanding and naming emotions can be powerful. But as one progresses, it's crucial to delve deeper, understanding the nuances, triggers, and the interplay between different emotions.

The Importance of Continued Practice

1. **Building Resilience**: Just as muscles strengthen with regular exercise, consistent EI practice helps build emotional resilience. This resilience helps individuals bounce back from setbacks, manage stress, and maintain mental well-being.

2. **Enhancing Relationships**: Continual EI practice fosters healthier relationships. Being attuned to one's emotions and those of others helps in building empathy, understanding, and effective communication.

3. **Professional Growth**: The corporate world is increasingly recognizing the value of EI. Continuous cultivation can lead to better leadership skills, teamwork, and adaptability in changing work environments.

4. **Personal Well-being**: At its core, emotional intelligence is deeply linked to one's overall well-being. Regular practice can lead to improved mental health, better decision-making skills, and a more fulfilled life.

5. **Mitigating Negative Patterns**: Over time, unchecked emotional patterns can become ingrained and automatic. Regular reflection and practice help identify and rectify these patterns before they become detrimental habits.

Conclusion

The journey of emotional intelligence is lifelong. It doesn't have an endpoint, but rather offers milestones of growth, understanding, and depth. In a world that often emphasizes intellectual achievements and tangible accomplishments, the journey of EI reminds us of the profound impact of the intangible. By recognizing the ongoing nature of this journey and dedicating oneself to its continuous practice, individuals can lead a life of balance, understanding, and profound connection with oneself and others.

Course 15, Section 2
Strategies for Developing Emotional Intelligence

Introduction

Emotional Intelligence (EI) development isn't merely about recognizing its importance, but actively adopting strategies to hone it. Cultivating EI is akin to nurturing a garden; it requires attention, tools, and consistent care. Below, we delve into several strategies that aid in the consistent nurturing of emotional intelligence.

1. Mindfulness

Description: Mindfulness is the practice of being present, attentive, and fully engaged in the current moment. It involves observing your thoughts, feelings, and sensations without judgment.

EI Connection: Practicing mindfulness fosters self-awareness, one of the cornerstones of EI. It allows individuals to recognize their emotions as they arise, understand their origin, and respond rather than react.

Implementation: Begin with short, daily mindfulness meditation sessions. Even just a few minutes of focused breathing, paying attention to the sensation of the air entering and leaving the nostrils, can be a starting point. Over time, one can also practice mindfulness during daily activities such as eating, walking, or listening.

2. Journaling

Description: Journaling involves recording thoughts, feelings, and experiences in a diary or digital platform.

EI Connection: By writing down emotions and experiences, individuals can gain clarity, understand emotional triggers, and process feelings in a constructive manner. It's a form of self-reflection that deepens emotional understanding.

Implementation: Dedicate a few minutes each day or several times a week to jot down your feelings, experiences, and reactions. Over time, patterns may emerge that offer insights into emotional behaviors and triggers.

3. Regular Self-Reflection

Description: Self-reflection involves taking the time to think about one's actions, decisions, and emotions in order to gain insight.

EI Connection: Reflecting on one's experiences aids in emotional self-awareness and regulation. It allows for the recognition of emotional patterns, understanding their implications, and adapting behaviors for improved outcomes.

Implementation: Set aside dedicated time for reflection. This could be during a quiet morning routine, an evening walk, or through practices like meditation. Ask yourself questions like, "How did I handle that situation?", "What could I have done differently?", or "Why did that comment affect me so deeply?"

4. Seeking Feedback from Others

Description: This involves actively seeking input from colleagues, friends, or mentors about one's emotional behaviors and responses.

EI Connection: Others often see facets of ourselves that we may overlook. By seeking feedback, individuals can gain a broader perspective on their emotional conduct, helping to improve interpersonal relationships and self-regulation.

Implementation: Create a safe environment for feedback by asking open-ended questions such as, "Can you tell me how you felt when I said that?" or "How do you perceive my reaction during meetings?" Be open to feedback without being defensive and use it constructively to guide personal growth.

Conclusion

Developing Emotional Intelligence is an ongoing process that requires commitment, introspection, and consistent effort. By incorporating strategies such as mindfulness, journaling, regular self-reflection, and seeking feedback, individuals can foster a deeper understanding of their emotional landscape and navigate life's challenges with greater awareness and skill. As with any skill, the more one practices, the more adept they become. So, the journey of EI development is not just about the destination but the rich insights and growth that come along the way.

Course 15, Section 3

Exercises to Enhance Emotional Intelligence

Introduction

Building emotional intelligence (EI) is much like strengthening a muscle; regular exercises can hone and enhance one's ability to understand, use, and manage emotions effectively. Let's delve into some pivotal exercises that can be easily integrated into daily routines for the continual development of EI.

1. Emotion Regulation Exercises

Description: Emotion regulation exercises help individuals understand, accept, and manage their emotions. They promote emotional resilience and allow for a balanced emotional response to different situations.

Example Exercise - The 'Pause & Reflect' Method

> 1. Whenever you experience a strong emotion (like anger or frustration), pause for a moment before reacting.
>
> 2. Take three deep breaths.
>
> 3. Ask yourself: "What am I feeling right now? Why might I be feeling this way?"
>
> 4. Decide on a constructive way to express or deal with the emotion.

By doing this regularly, one cultivates the habit of introspection before action, leading to more balanced and controlled reactions.

2. Empathy Practice

Description: Empathy is the ability to understand and share the feelings of another. Empathy practices help individuals step into others' shoes, promoting understanding and compassionate interactions.

Example Exercise - The 'Empathy Journal'

    1. Each day, think of a situation where someone else showed emotion (a coworker seeming stressed, a friend being excited, etc.).

    2. Write down the emotion you perceived and why you think they might have felt that way.

    3. Reflect on a time you felt the same way and jot down how you wanted others to respond to you.

    4. Use this understanding to inform future interactions, making a conscious effort to offer the response you would've desired.

This exercise encourages a deeper understanding of shared human experiences, fostering genuine connections.

3. Active Listening Activities

Description: Active listening is fully concentrating, understanding, and responding to what someone else is saying. It's an essential component of effective communication and is crucial for understanding others' emotional states.

Example Exercise - 'Repeat & Reflect'

    1. In your next conversation, focus solely on the speaker. Avoid formulating your response while they're still talking.

    2. Once they've finished speaking, repeat back a brief summary of what they said to ensure you've understood.

    3. Reflect on the emotions they might be feeling and validate them, e.g., "It sounds like you're feeling overwhelmed because of the tight deadline. That's understandable."

This practice underscores the importance of truly hearing another person and offering validation, which can strengthen interpersonal relationships.

Conclusion

Each of these exercises provides a tangible approach to nurturing different aspects of emotional intelligence. Incorporating them into daily routines can lead to enhanced self-awareness, improved relationships, and a deeper understanding of oneself and others. As with any practice, consistency is key. Over time, these exercises will not only become second nature but will also significantly boost one's EI, paving the way for more harmonious interactions and a richer emotional life.

Course 15, Section 4
Overcoming Obstacles to Growth in Emotional Intelligence

Introduction

As with any personal development journey, growing one's emotional intelligence (EI) is not without its challenges. Several obstacles can hinder this growth and recognizing them is the first step toward effectively navigating, and ultimately overcoming them. Below, we explore some common obstacles and offer strategies to counteract them.

1. Lack of Self-awareness

Description: Being unaware of one's own emotions or the reasons behind them can be a significant hindrance to EI development.

Strategy to Overcome:

• **Regular Self-reflection**: Allocate a few minutes daily to introspect on the day's emotions, reactions, and triggers. This can help in identifying patterns and understanding oneself better.

• **Feedback Seeking**: Ask close friends, family, or colleagues for feedback on emotional reactions in specific situations. This external perspective can provide new insights.

2. Defensiveness

Description: Taking constructive feedback or criticism personally can impede emotional growth.

Strategy to Overcome:

• **Neutralization Technique**: Whenever you feel criticized or defensive, pause, and try to detach yourself from the situation. View the feedback as information, not as a personal attack.

• **Open-mindedness**: Foster a growth mindset. Understand that feedback is a tool for improvement, not an indication of failure.

3. Overwhelm with Strong Emotions

Description: Some individuals may feel overwhelmed by intense emotions, making it challenging to react rationally or empathetically.

Strategy to Overcome:

• Emotion Labeling: By naming the emotion (e.g., "I'm feeling anxious"), you can create a psychological distance and better manage the feeling.

• Mindfulness Practices: Engaging in mindfulness or meditation can help center oneself and provide clarity in emotionally charged situations.

4. Difficulty in Empathizing with Others

Description: Struggling to understand or resonate with others' emotions can hinder relational aspects of EI.

Strategy to Overcome:

• **Active Listening**: Prioritize listening over speaking. This can help in genuinely understanding others' perspectives.

• **Role-playing**: Engage in exercises where you place yourself in another person's situation. This can aid in developing a deeper sense of empathy.

5. Fear of Vulnerability

Description: Many people associate vulnerability with weakness, leading them to hide their true feelings or avoid emotional topics.

Strategy to Overcome:

> • Gradual Exposure: Start by sharing small emotional experiences with trusted individuals, gradually working up to more profound emotions.

> • Educate Yourself: Understand that vulnerability can be a strength. Reading books or attending workshops on the topic can be enlightening.

6. Cultural or Societal Norms

Description: In certain cultures, and societies, emotional expression might be suppressed or viewed negatively.

Strategy to Overcome:

> • Find Safe Spaces: Seek out groups or environments where emotional expression is encouraged and valued.

> • Awareness and Education: Understand cultural norms but educate yourself and, when possible, others about the value of emotional intelligence and its universal importance.

Conclusion

While the journey of developing emotional intelligence may have its hurdles, it is essential to remember that growth often comes from facing and overcoming challenges. By recognizing these obstacles and employing the mentioned strategies, one can steadily progress on the path of emotional growth, leading to richer personal and interpersonal experiences.

Course 15, Section 5
Practical Application and Long-term Growth

Introduction

While understanding the theoretical components of emotional intelligence is foundational, its real value emerges through daily application. This section offers guidance on incorporating EI strategies into everyday life and creating a long-term plan for sustainable emotional growth.

1. Daily Application of Emotional Intelligence

• **Mindfulness Meditation**: Begin your day with a 10-minute mindfulness meditation. This helps in centering oneself and increases self-awareness of emotions throughout the day.

• **Emotion Check-ins**: Schedule three emotion check-ins during your day (morning, mid-day, evening). Recognize, label, and reflect on the emotions you feel. This enhances self-awareness and self-regulation.

• **Active Listening**: Make it a goal in every conversation to truly listen. This means not formulating a response while the other person is speaking but truly hearing and understanding their point of view.

• **Empathy Practice**: In interactions with others, try to put yourself in their shoes, especially if their viewpoint or emotions differ from yours. This not only builds relationships but also strengthens your empathetic abilities.

• **Reflect on Feedback**: Whenever you receive feedback, take time to reflect on it, especially if it's emotionally charged. Approach it with a growth mindset, seeking to understand and grow from it.

2. Creating a Personal EI Development Plan

Step 1: Self-assessment

Before making any plan, you need to know where you stand. Use EI assessments or quizzes available online or seek feedback from trusted colleagues or friends.

Step 2: Set Clear Objectives

Based on your self-assessment, identify areas that need improvement. For instance, if self-regulation is a challenge, make it an objective to manage emotional reactions better in high-pressure situations.

Step 3: Choose Strategies and Techniques

Pick strategies from this course that align with your objectives. If you're working on empathy, strategies like active listening and role-playing could be beneficial.

Step 4: Practice Regularly

Consistency is crucial. Dedicate time daily or weekly to practice these strategies, be it through mindfulness exercises, journaling, or seeking regular feedback.

Step 5: Seek a Mentor or Coach

A mentor who excels in EI can provide guidance, offer feedback, and share their experiences, helping to accelerate your growth.

Step 6: Evaluate and Adjust

Every month or quarter, reassess your emotional intelligence growth. Celebrate the areas of improvement and adjust your strategies for areas that still need work.

3. **Long-term Commitment**

• **Continued Learning**: The field of EI is vast and ever evolving. Regularly attend workshops, read books, or take courses to keep updated.

• **Teach Others**: One of the best ways to learn is to teach. Share your knowledge and experiences with others. This reinforces your understanding and establishes you as an advocate for EI.

• **Maintain an EI Journal**: Dedicate a journal to track your emotional journey. Note down challenging situations, your reactions, your reflections, and growth over time.

• **Join EI Groups or Forums**: Being part of a community that values EI can be a significant boost. Share experiences, seek advice, and learn from diverse perspectives.

Conclusion

Emotional intelligence, like any skill, flourishes with consistent practice and application. By integrating EI practices into daily life and committing to a structured development plan, individuals can foster their emotional growth, leading to enhanced personal and professional relationships and a greater understanding of oneself and others.

Supplementary Material: A Collage Documentary

My EI Journey

The scene fades in from black, showing a bustling city street. We hear ambient sounds - car horns, distant chatter, footsteps. The title, "My EI Journey," appears on the screen.

Narrator (V.O.): In the heart of our daily lives, amidst the noise, the chaos, and the routines, there lies a silent journey, often overlooked. Today, we delve into the intimate world of individuals who have transformed their lives by embracing Emotional Intelligence.

Cut to a cozy living room. We see Jessica, a mid-30s business professional, sitting on her couch.

Jessica: Before diving into EI, I was on the brink of burnout. Tight deadlines, team conflicts, family pressures. I was juggling it all, but with every ball that I added, I felt another piece of me slipping away.

Flashback montage of Jessica looking stressed at work, having heated arguments with colleagues, and looking overwhelmed at home.

Jessica: I started with mindfulness meditation. Initially, it was just ten minutes a day. But those ten minutes of quiet reflection...they changed everything.

Cut to a serene park scene. We see Jessica meditating, her face calm.

Jessica: Through mindfulness, I discovered my triggers, understood my reactions, and slowly started responding instead of reacting.

We transitioned to a café setting. Robert, a schoolteacher in his late 40s, takes a sip of his coffee.

Robert: I've always been an active listener, but EI taught me about the depth of empathy. It's more than just listening. It's feeling, understanding, and connecting on a profound level.

Flashback to Robert in a classroom setting, listening intently to a student.

Robert: One of my students was constantly disruptive. But instead of reprimanding him outright, I chose to actively listen. Turned out, he was battling issues at home. That empathetic approach changed our student-teacher dynamic entirely.

We moved to an apartment, where Anita, a young artist in her 20s, is painting.

Anita: Journaling! That's my go-to EI practice. Every emotion, every turmoil, every joy finds its way into my journal. It's my safe space.

The camera focuses on her diary, filled with intricate details, sketches, and writings.

Anita: Through journaling, I started recognizing patterns in my emotions. On canvas, I wasn't just painting colors but my emotions, raw and unfiltered.

A scenic beach at sunset. Mark, a retired army veteran, looks at the horizon.

Mark: The army taught me discipline, but EI taught me self-awareness. When I returned from service, I struggled with PTSD. Emotion regulation exercises became my anchor.

Flashback of Mark attending therapy, practicing deep breathing exercises.

Mark: Every time I felt an emotional wave, I employed these exercises. It didn't eliminate the trauma, but it gave me control, understanding, and a way to navigate through it.

The camera returns to the city street, but now we see it differently - people are more engaged, there's laughter, understanding, and connections.

Narrator (V.O.): Emotional Intelligence isn't just about self-awareness or managing stress. It's a journey of understanding oneself and others, of building bridges where walls once stood, and of creating a world filled with empathy and understanding.

Cut to a montage of all the individuals - Jessica practicing mindfulness, Robert listening to his student, Anita painting, and Mark meditating on the beach.

Narrator (V.O.): As we have seen, the journey of EI is personal yet universal. It's challenging yet transformative. And for those willing to embark on this journey, the destination is a life filled with deeper connections, understanding, and peace.

Fade to black with the words: "Your EI Journey Begins Today."

The End.

Parting Thoughts

Ensure that learners are encouraged to reflect and put into practice the learned strategies. These real-world applications and personal experiences are critical in embedding the learning for long-term benefit.

Course 16
Conclusion
Emotional Intelligence in Everyday Life

Learning Objectives for Course 16

1. Review and summarize key points from the entire course.

2. Understand the applications of emotional intelligence in everyday life.

3. Reflect on personal growth throughout the course and plan for the journey ahead.

Course 16, Section 1

Recap of the Journey

Course 1: Introduction to Emotional Intelligence

- Unveiled the realm of emotional intelligence and its multifaceted importance.
- Delved into the key components that shape our emotional intelligence.
- Set the pace for the curriculum, outlining our journey and objectives.

Course 2: Understanding Emotions

- Dissected the essence of emotions and their significance in our lives.
- Delved into the mechanics of emotions – from triggers to processes.
- Emphasized how emotions play a crucial role in influencing our daily actions and decisions.

Courses 3 & 4: Emotional Self-Awareness Parts 1 & 2

- Defined the importance of recognizing and naming our own emotions.
- Introduced emotional triggers, their impact, and strategies for self-awareness.

Courses 5, 6 & 7: Emotional Self-Regulation Parts 1, 2 & 3

- Dived deeper into understanding emotional triggers and techniques for healthy emotional responses.
- Explored the avenues of self-soothing and cognitive reappraisal.
- Discussed cognitive distortions and their influence on our emotional world.

Course 8: Understanding Others' Emotions – Empathy

- Delved into the world of empathy and its paramount significance in emotional intelligence.

- Discussed techniques to home in on and identify emotions of others effectively.

- Emphasized the art of empathetic listening and response.

Courses 9, 10 & 11: Interpersonal Relationships Parts 1, 2 & 3

- Recognized the role of emotional intelligence in fostering effective communication and handling conflicts.

- Discussed the significance of setting healthy boundaries in relationships.

- Ventured into the world of challenging social scenarios and the utility of emotional intelligence in navigating them.

Courses 12, 13 & 14: Emotional Intelligence in the Workplace Parts 1, 2 & 3

- Established the irreplaceable role of emotional intelligence in teamwork, leadership, and managing workplace stress.

- Focused on the strategies that enable us to use emotional intelligence to its full potential in our professional lives.

- Delved into practical scenarios highlighting how emotional intelligence can be a game-changer in managing stress and preventing burnout.

Courses 15: Developing Your Emotional Intelligence – Practice and Growth

- Focused on the never-ending journey of emotional intelligence growth and the importance of continued practice.

- Introduced strategies and daily exercises to continually hone our emotional intelligence.

Conclusion

The journey we embarked on through this curriculum has been profound and transformative. Emotional intelligence is more than just understanding emotions; it's about mastering them, both within and around us. It's about recognizing emotions, understanding their origin, managing them, and empathizing with others. From personal relationships to the workplace, the influence of emotional intelligence is pervasive.

Emotional intelligence isn't a one-time lesson but a lifelong journey. As we integrate these principles into our everyday life, we will witness a remarkable transformation in how we interact with the world, handle challenges, build relationships, and lead teams. With the foundational knowledge and skills gained from this curriculum, you are now equipped to face life's multifaceted scenarios with enhanced emotional aptitude.

Course 16, Section 2
Emotional Intelligence in Everyday Life

Emotional intelligence (EI) transcends the confines of textbooks and theoretical discussions. It manifests vividly in our everyday experiences, significantly influencing our interactions, decisions, and overall well-being. Let's explore seven practical scenarios demonstrating the application of EI in daily life:

1. **Handling Criticism at Work**

Scenario: Jane, a manager, receives feedback from her boss that her recent project presentation lacked depth.

EI Application: Instead of reacting defensively or feeling defeated, Jane takes a moment to process her emotions. She uses her self-awareness to understand her initial disappointment and self-regulation to not let that emotion cloud her judgment. Later, she approaches her boss with genuine curiosity, seeking specifics on where she could improve, turning the critique into a learning opportunity.

2. **Resolving Conflicts in Personal Relationships**

Scenario: Mike and Ella, a married couple, find themselves frequently arguing about household chores.

EI Application: Recognizing the recurring pattern, Ella initiates a calm conversation, practicing empathetic listening. She understands that Mike feels overwhelmed with work pressures. They both use their emotional awareness to express feelings and decide on a shared chores calendar, diffusing tension and reinforcing their bond.

3. Navigating Team Dynamics

Scenario: In a team meeting, two members engage in a heated argument about project direction.

EI Application: Sarah, a team member, intervenes by acknowledging the emotions in the room. She utilizes her interpersonal skills to redirect the conversation towards the core objective and proposes a collaborative solution. Her emotional understanding and regulation act as a harmonizing force, turning a potential clash into a productive dialogue.

4. Managing Stressful Commutes

Scenario: Everyday traffic jams make Raj's commute to work highly stressful, often setting a negative tone for the rest of his day.

EI Application: Raj decides to use this time constructively. He starts listening to podcasts that boost his mood or expand his knowledge. By recognizing and addressing his stress triggers, he transforms a negative situation into a positive experience.

5. Dealing with Personal Loss

Scenario: After losing her pet, Maria is swamped with grief, struggling to cope with daily routines.

EI Application: Maria gives herself the space to grieve, practicing self-awareness. She also joins a support group, where she learns to channel her emotions constructively, like creating a memory book. Her ability to understand and process her emotions aids her healing journey.

6. Guiding Children's Emotions

- **Scenario**: Five-year-old Leo throws tantrums whenever he's asked to study.

- **EI Application**: Instead of scolding him, Leo's father, Sam, sits down to talk, trying to understand Leo's feelings. He realizes that Leo is struggling with a particular subject. Sam uses his emotional insight to address the root issue, offering help and making study time engaging, thereby reducing the tantrums.

7. Making Informed Decisions

Scenario: Tina gets a lucrative job offer from a company in another city.

EI Application: Instead of making a hasty decision, Tina introspects her emotions about relocating and the implications on her personal and professional life. She discusses with friends and mentors, using empathy to gauge their perspectives. Her emotionally informed approach ensures that she makes a choice aligned with both her feelings and her career goals.

Conclusion

In each of these scenarios, emotional intelligence acts as a compass, guiding individuals through the intricate maze of emotions and relationships. By recognizing, understanding, and managing emotions, and by being attuned to the feelings of others, we can navigate daily challenges more effectively, building stronger bonds and achieving greater well-being.

Course 16, Section 3
Personal Growth Reflection

Reflecting on personal growth is essential to cementing the lessons you've learned and identifying future developmental areas. As we conclude this emotional intelligence journey, let's delve into a series of reflective prompts. These will aid in evaluating your progress and setting the stage for continuous self-improvement:

1. **Self-awareness Assessment**:

• Recall a recent event where your emotions ran high. Were you able to recognize and name that emotion in the moment?

• How has your ability to recognize your emotional triggers changed since beginning this course?

• Are there still emotions you struggle to identify or understand in yourself? List them.

2. **Self-regulation Reflection**:

• Think about a situation where you successfully managed a strong emotional reaction. What techniques did you employ?

• Are there circumstances where you still find it challenging to control your emotional responses?

• How have the techniques from this course (like self-soothing or cognitive reappraisal) aided you in day-to-day situations?

3. **Empathy Evaluation**:

• Reflect on recent interactions with others. Are you more attuned to the emotions of those around you?

• Can you recall a situation where empathetic listening enhanced your understanding of another person's feelings?

• Are there specific scenarios or individuals with whom you still find it challenging to empathize?

4. **Interpersonal Skills Appraisal**:

• How have your relationships evolved since implementing the principles of emotional intelligence from this course?

• In what situations have you utilized EI to improve communication or resolve conflicts?

• Are there relationships or interactions where you believe further application of EI could be beneficial?

5. **Workplace Dynamics Observation**:

• Reflect on a recent team project or meeting. How did emotional intelligence play a role in collaboration and decision-making?

• How have you used EI principles in managing stress and preventing burnout in professional settings?

• Are there workplace situations where you feel you could have better applied EI concepts?

6. **Overall Personal Growth**:

• Which areas of emotional intelligence do you believe you've made the most progress in?

• Identify at least three significant lessons or techniques from the course that have had the most profound impact on your daily life.

• Are there specific sections of the course you feel you'd benefit from revisiting?

7. **Continued Development**:

• List three personal goals related to further enhancing your emotional intelligence in the coming months.

• Are there external resources (books, workshops, mentors) you plan to seek out for continued learning in emotional intelligence?

• How do you envision integrating the principles of emotional intelligence into your long-term personal and professional growth strategy?

Conclusion:

Personal reflection is a cornerstone of growth in emotional intelligence. By revisiting experiences and assessing your responses, you deepen your understanding and refine your techniques. It's a continuous journey, and this reflection is but a snapshot in time. Regular self-assessment, combined with the tools and knowledge from this course, will guide you towards a life rich in understanding, empathy, and emotional well-being.

Course 16, Section 4
Planning for the Future

Planning for the Future: Crafting Your Personal Development Plan

As we conclude our emotional intelligence curriculum, it's essential to remember that growth in EI doesn't end here. It's an ongoing journey, and to ensure that you keep progressing, a personal development plan will be your roadmap. Here's a structured activity to help you craft that plan:

Introduction:

Your personal development plan is a living document, one that will evolve with you. It's meant to provide clarity, set intentions, and track progress. It's a commitment to yourself to continue building on the foundation we've laid together on this course.

Activity: Creating Your Emotional Intelligence Development Plan

1. **Self-Assessment**:

Prompt: Where are you now in your EI journey? Example: "I've become more aware of my emotions, especially in stressful situations. However, I sometimes struggle with expressing empathy during conflicts."

2. **Vision Statement**:

Prompt: What do you hope to achieve regarding emotional intelligence in the future? Example: "I want to be a calm presence in challenging situations and understand others' emotions deeply to foster healthier relationships."

3. Short-Term Goals (1-3 months):

Prompt: List specific, measurable, achievable, relevant, and time-bound (SMART) goals you aim to achieve in the next few months. Example: "In the next two months, I will read one book on emotional intelligence and practice active listening in all of my conversations."

4. Medium-Term Goals (4-12 months):

Prompt: Considering your vision, what milestones would you like to reach within a year? Example: "By the end of the year, I want to attend two workshops on conflict resolution and implement learned techniques in my workplace."

5. Long-Term Goals (1 year and beyond):

Prompt: Think about the bigger picture. Where do you see your emotional intelligence journey leading you in the years to come? Example: "In the next three years, I aim to lead emotional intelligence training sessions at my workplace, sharing my experiences and promoting an empathetic culture."

6. Resources & Tools:

Prompt: What resources (books, courses, workshops) will you use to achieve these goals? Example: "I'll read 'Emotional Intelligence 2.0' by Travis Bradberry and attend the annual Emotional Intelligence Summit."

7. Regular Check-ins:

Prompt: How often will you review and adjust this plan? Example: "I will revisit my development plan every three months to assess progress, celebrate achievements, and make necessary adjustments."

8. Support System:

Prompt: Who can support you on this journey? Think of mentors, peers, or groups that can provide guidance, encouragement, or feedback. Example: "I will join the local Emotional Intelligence Meetup group and seek regular feedback from my close friend, who's also focused on EI development."

9. **Challenges & Solutions**:

Prompt: Anticipate potential obstacles that might hinder your progress and think of strategies to overcome them. Example: "One challenge might be finding time for regular reflection. To counter this, I will set aside 10 minutes every evening for journaling."

10. **Reflection & Celebration**:

Prompt: How will you celebrate your achievements and learn from areas of improvement? Example: "For every short-term goal achieved, I'll treat myself to a day out. For larger milestones, maybe a weekend getaway. If I face setbacks, I'll consult my support system for perspective and adjust my strategies."

Conclusion:

The journey to honing emotional intelligence is continuous and evolving. This personal development plan serves as a guide, ensuring that the knowledge and insights gained from this curriculum find practical and lasting application in your daily life. Remember, growth isn't linear; there will be challenges, but with commitment and this roadmap, you're well-equipped to navigate your EI journey towards a brighter, more emotionally intelligent future.

Course 16, Section 5

Farewell Message

Farewell Message

Continuing Your Emotional Intelligence Odyssey

Dear Emotional Intelligence Student,

As we draw the curtains on our shared journey through the vast landscape of emotional intelligence, it's essential to remember that, like all meaningful quests, the road does not end here. Instead, it continues, winding and branching out, filled with countless opportunities to learn, grow, and transform.

Emotional Intelligence, as we've come to understand, isn't a destination; it's a lifelong journey. And, like all journeys, its essence lies not in the endpoint but in the experiences, we gather, the challenges we overcome, and the relationships we nurture along the way.

Every emotion you encounter, every connection you forge, and every challenge you face is an opportunity to hone your EI. Life will continually present scenarios—some familiar, some new—that will test and shape your emotional capacities. Embrace them. Let them be your teachers, for they are the real-life lessons that no classroom can wholly replicate.

Remember the times during this course when a concept seemed daunting, or an exercise felt challenging? Yet, here you are, having traversed through, growing not just in knowledge but in emotional depth and understanding. That growth is a testament to your resilience, your commitment, and your potential.

Keep the fire of curiosity alive. Continue to reflect, to question, to connect. Delve deeper into yourself, expand your horizons, and never stop seeking. Emotional intelligence, much like a well-tended garden, flourishes with consistent care, mindfulness, and practice.

In times of doubt or difficulty, I encourage you to revisit the lessons, exercises, and reflections we've shared. Let them be your guiding light, reminding you of your capabilities and the beautiful journey ahead. Share your insights and experiences with others; be a beacon for those who embark on this journey after you.

As we bid farewell, remember that every ending is but a new beginning. The skills and knowledge you've gained are tools in your kit, but your heart—the compassion, empathy, and understanding it holds—is your true compass.

Stay brave, stay curious, and most importantly, stay connected—to yourself and to the world around you. Here's to the countless emotional adventures ahead and the richer, more insightful soul you're evolving into with each passing day.

With heartfelt warmth and boundless encouragement,

Dr. Rea Prado

Dr. Rea Prado

Jessica@pradoic.com

https://pradoic.info/

linkedin.com/in/jessicareaprado

Supplementary Material

Everyday EI: A Collection of Parables or Stories

More from this Publisher:

The "**Accessible Emotional Intelligence Series**" is a supplemental series of 5 books created with this curriculum in mind. Each book has a selection of inspirational and educational short stories to guide you through tough interpersonal challenges that we all face every day. You can use this series as a reference as you continue your emotional intelligence journey. There are almost 300 short stories in the series, usually only two pages each so they are a quick read, providing real-life examples of challenges in which a well-chosen emotional intelligence approach creates a dramatic change in the outcome compared to what all of us have personally witnessed at one time or another. The books in this series are listed on the last page of this book, and are available from Amazon in kindle, paperback, and hardcover formats, as well as many other places you'll find great books.

Parting Thought

Ensure to remind learners to continue practicing their EI skills and reflect on their progress regularly. The more they use these skills in real-life scenarios, the more they'll be able to benefit from their emotional intelligence.

Glossary of Emotional Intelligence Terms

Acceptance: The willingness to embrace and acknowledge reality, including oneself and others, without judgment or resistance.

Accountability: Taking responsibility for one's actions, decisions, and their consequences, both personally and professionally.

Active Listening: Listening attentively and responding to others in a way that improves mutual understanding and fosters effective communication.

Adaptability: The ability to adjust and respond positively to changing circumstances and challenges.

Advocacy: Speaking up and supporting a cause or belief to bring about positive change or defend the rights of others.

Affect: The experience of feeling or emotion, often referring to the outward display of emotions.

Alexithymia: A personality construct characterized by the subclinical inability to identify and describe emotions experienced by oneself or others.

Allyship: An active and supportive relationship between individuals or groups, particularly with regard to advocating for marginalized communities.

Anger: An intense emotional state often associated with feelings of displeasure, hostility, and frustration.

Anxiety: A state of unease or apprehension, typically about future uncertainties or potential threats.

Assertiveness: The quality of being self-assured and confident without being aggressive, often used in expressing needs or boundaries.

Attachment: Emotional bond or connection formed between individuals, often observed in close relationships.

Authenticity: The quality of being genuine and true to oneself, embracing one's values, beliefs, and emotions.

Balance: A state of equilibrium and harmony in various aspects of life, including emotions, work, and personal relationships.

Belonging: The feeling of being connected and accepted as a part of a group or community.

Boundaries: Clear and healthy limits set to protect one's physical, emotional, and mental well-being in relationships and interactions.

Bravery: The courage to confront fears, challenges, or difficulties with determination and resilience.

Burnout: A state of emotional, physical, and mental exhaustion caused by prolonged stress or overwhelming work demands.

Calmness: A state of tranquility and inner peace, often achieved through relaxation and emotional regulation.

Caregiving: Providing support, assistance, and care for others, particularly in times of need or vulnerability.

Catharsis: The process of releasing strong or repressed emotions through various forms of expression, such as art or communication.

Change: The process of transition or transformation from one state to another, often involving adjustments and adaptation.

Childhood Trauma: Adverse experiences or events during childhood that can have long-lasting emotional and psychological effects.

Choice: The act of making a decision or selecting an option from different possibilities.

Clarity: The quality of being clear, well-defined, and easily understood, often related to thoughts and communication.

Closure: A sense of resolution or finality regarding a situation or relationship, allowing emotional healing and moving forward.

Cognitive Empathy: The ability to understand and intellectually grasp another person's perspective or mental state.

Collaboration: Working together with others to achieve common goals, often involving open communication and cooperation.

Communication: The exchange of information, thoughts, and feelings between individuals through verbal and non-verbal means.

Compassion: The feeling of understanding and caring about another person's distress, accompanied by a desire to alleviate their suffering.

Compassionate Listening: Listening to others in a way that provides emotional healing for the speaker, demonstrating empathy and understanding.

Compromise: The act of finding a middle ground or mutual agreement in a situation where different parties have conflicting interests.

Conflict Resolution: The method and processes involved in facilitating the peaceful ending of conflict, often through negotiation and communication.

Connection: The bond and sense of relatedness between individuals, often involving emotional intimacy and mutual understanding.

Consistency: The quality of being reliable, predictable, and maintaining stability in thoughts, emotions, and actions.

Coping Mechanisms: Adaptive strategies and behaviors used to handle and manage stress, adversity, or challenging situations.

Courage: The mental and emotional strength to face difficult situations or challenges, often despite fear or uncertainty.

Creativity: The ability to think imaginatively and generate original ideas, often expressed through various forms of artistic expression.

Critical Self-Reflection: The process of objectively examining one's thoughts, actions, and emotions to gain insight and personal growth.

Cultural Sensitivity: The awareness and respect for different cultural norms, beliefs, and practices, promoting understanding and inclusivity.

Curiosity: A strong desire to learn, explore, and understand new information and experiences.

Decision-Making: The process of selecting a course of action from various options, often involving analysis and evaluation.

De-escalation: The process of calming or reducing tension and conflict in a situation to prevent escalation.

Dependence: Reliance on others for support, assistance, or emotional validation.

Depression: A mood disorder characterized by persistent feelings of sadness, hopelessness, and a lack of interest or pleasure in activities.

Disagreement: A difference of opinion or viewpoint between individuals or groups.

Disappointment: The feeling of sadness or dissatisfaction resulting from unmet expectations or hopes.

Disconnection: A sense of being emotionally or socially disconnected from others or oneself.

Display Rules: Social and cultural norms that guide emotional expression and behavior in different contexts.

Distress Tolerance: The ability to manage actual or perceived emotional distress in a healthy and adaptive manner.

Diversity: The variety and differences among individuals, including race, ethnicity, gender, culture, and beliefs.

Emotion Differentiation: The ability to make fine-grained distinctions between different emotions, identifying and labeling them accurately.

Emotion Dissonance: The conflict between experienced emotions and those expressed to comply with social or cultural display rules.

Emotion Regulation: The ability to manage and control one's emotions in different situations, promoting emotional well-being.

Emotional Agility: The ability to navigate life's twists and turns with self-acceptance, clear-sightedness, and an open mind.

Emotional Boundaries: Personal limits and guidelines set to protect one's emotional well-being in relationships and interactions.

Emotional Coaching: Guiding individuals to recognize and understand their emotions and using this awareness to manage behavior and relationships.

Emotional Competence: The ability to control and manage one's emotions for personal growth and effective communication.

Emotional Contagion: The phenomenon of having one person's emotions directly trigger similar emotions in others.

Emotional Empathy: The ability to share and understand another person's feelings or emotions, often leading to a compassionate response.

Emotional Exhaustion: A state of depletion and fatigue resulting from prolonged emotional stress or demands.

Emotional Expression: The process of communicating one's emotional state through verbal and non-verbal means.

Emotional Granularity: The ability to specifically and clearly identify one's own emotions, including subtle variations.

Emotional Hijacking: An instance in which an individual's rational thinking is overpowered by their emotional response.

Emotional Intelligence (EI): A person's ability to recognize, understand, manage, and use their own emotions and those of others effectively.

Emotional Invalidation: The process of rejecting or ignoring someone's emotional experiences, leading to feelings of dismissal or worthlessness.

Emotional Labor: The process of managing feelings and expressions as part of a job role, particularly in customer service or caregiving.

Emotional Literacy: The ability to recognize and understand the emotions of oneself and others, often leading to effective communication.

Emotional Resilience: The ability to adapt to stressful situations and recover from adversity, maintaining emotional well-being.

Emotional Schemas: The cognitive structures that individuals use to make sense of and interpret their emotions.

Emotional Vulnerability: The state of being open to emotional hurt or pain, often associated with authenticity and courage.

Emotion-Focused Coping: A type of stress management that aims to reduce negative emotional responses associated with stress.

Empathy: The ability to understand and share the feelings of others, often leading to compassionate and supportive behavior.

Empowerment: The process of supporting and enabling individuals to take control of their lives and make positive changes.

Encouragement: Providing support, praise, and motivation to others to boost their confidence and well-being.

Energy Management: The practice of efficiently using and regulating one's physical, emotional, and mental energy.

Engagement: The level of involvement, enthusiasm, and interest in an activity or relationship.

Equality: The belief and practice of treating all individuals with fairness and impartiality, regardless of their background or characteristics.

Ethics: Principles and moral values that guide decision-making and behavior, particularly in professional contexts.

Expressiveness: The degree and manner in which emotions are outwardly displayed through facial expressions, body language, and vocal tone.

Family Dynamics: The patterns and interactions within a family system, including communication, roles, and emotional connections.

Fear: An emotional response to perceived threats or dangers, often leading to a fight-or-flight reaction.

Feedback: Information, opinions, or evaluations provided to individuals to promote learning, growth, and improvement.

Fixed Mindset: The belief that one's abilities, intelligence, and talents are fixed traits, leading to resistance to change or improvement.

Flexibility: The ability to adapt and adjust to changing circumstances, opinions, or expectations.

Flow: A state of complete absorption and focus on an activity, resulting in a loss of sense of time and self.

Forgiveness: The act of letting go of resentment and granting pardon to oneself or others for past offenses.

Friendship: A close and supportive relationship between individuals characterized by mutual trust and affection.

Frustration: A feeling of annoyance or dissatisfaction resulting from obstacles or unmet needs.

Fulfillment: A sense of satisfaction, contentment, and accomplishment from achieving personal goals and meaningful experiences.

Generosity: The willingness to give and provide support, resources, or kindness to others.

Gratitude: The quality of being thankful and appreciative, often for the kindness and generosity of others.

Grief: The emotional response to loss or bereavement, often involving feelings of sadness, sorrow, and longing.

Grit: A trait based on an individual's perseverance of effort combined with passion for a long-term goal.

Growth Mindset: The belief that one's abilities and intelligence can be developed with time, effort, and dedication.

Guilt: A feeling of remorse or responsibility for a perceived wrongdoing or harm caused to others.

Handling Criticism: The ability to receive and process feedback or criticism constructively, without becoming defensive or upset.

Healing: The process of recovering and restoring physical, emotional, or psychological well-being after experiencing difficulties or trauma.

Healthy Boundaries: Establishing and maintaining appropriate limits in relationships to protect one's emotional and physical well-being.

Honesty: The quality of being truthful, transparent, and sincere in thoughts, words, and actions.

Hope: A positive and optimistic attitude toward the future, often involving a belief in the possibility of positive outcomes.

Identity: The sense of self and individuality, formed by personal beliefs, values, and experiences.

Inclusivity: The practice of embracing and involving all individuals, regardless of their differences or backgrounds.

Independence: The ability to function and make decisions autonomously, without excessive reliance on others.

Insecurity: A feeling of uncertainty or lack of confidence in oneself or one's abilities.

Integrity: The adherence to moral and ethical principles, demonstrating honesty and consistency in actions and values.

Intention: A deliberate and purposeful direction of thoughts and actions toward a specific goal or outcome.

Interpersonal Skills: The ability to interact effectively and harmoniously with others, often involving communication and empathy.

Intrapersonal Skills: The ability to understand and manage one's own emotions, thoughts, and behaviors.

Jealousy: A feeling of envy or resentment toward another person's possessions, achievements, or relationships.

Joy: A feeling of delight, happiness, or satisfaction, often experienced in response to positive events or experiences.

Kindness: The quality of being considerate, compassionate, and benevolent toward others.

Leadership: The ability to guide and influence others toward a common goal or vision, often involving inspiration and motivation.

Listening: The act of paying attention to and actively comprehending verbal and non-verbal communication from others.

Locus of Control: The degree to which people believe that they, as opposed to external forces, have control over the outcome of events in their lives.

Loneliness: The feeling of isolation or disconnection from others, often resulting in emotional distress.

Love: A deep and affectionate feeling of care, attachment, and concern for oneself or others.

Managing Expectations: Setting realistic and achievable expectations for oneself and others to reduce disappointment and frustration.

Meditation: The practice of focusing attention and calming the mind to achieve mental clarity and relaxation.

Mental Health: The state of emotional, psychological, and social well-being, often involving coping with stress and managing emotions.

Mindfulness: The psychological process of bringing one's attention to experiences occurring in the present moment without judgment.

Mindset: The established set of attitudes held by someone, often influencing behavior and decision-making.

Mood: A temporary state of mind or feeling, often influenced by emotions and external factors.

Motivation: The drive and desire to pursue goals, often influenced by internal and external factors.

Negotiation: The process of communication and compromise between individuals to reach mutually satisfactory agreements.

Neuroplasticity: The ability of the brain to form and reorganize synaptic connections, especially in response to learning or experience.

Non-Verbal Communication: Communicating feelings or ideas without words, using things like body language, facial expressions, and tone of voice.

Nurturing: Providing care, support, and encouragement to foster growth and development in oneself or others.

Open-Mindedness: The willingness to consider new ideas, perspectives, and information without prejudice or bias.

Optimism: Hopefulness and confidence about the future or successful outcome of something.

Overcoming Adversity: Successfully navigating and surmounting challenges, difficulties, or setbacks in life.

Overwhelm: Feeling excessively burdened or stressed by a situation or multiple tasks.

Patience: The ability to remain calm and composed in the face of delays, challenges, or provocation.

Perceived Emotional Intelligence (PEI): An individual's perception of their ability to recognize and understand emotions in themselves and others.

Perseverance: The determination and persistence to continue striving toward goals, despite obstacles or setbacks.

Perspective: A particular way of viewing or understanding a situation or concept, influenced by individual beliefs and experiences.

Perspective Taking: The act of perceiving a situation or understanding a concept from an alternative point of view.

Pessimism: The tendency to see the worst aspect of things or believe that the worst will happen.

Positive Psychology: The study of happiness and well-being, focusing on factors that contribute to a fulfilling and meaningful life.

Positivity: An optimistic and positive attitude toward oneself and others, often promoting resilience and emotional well-being.

Post-Traumatic Growth: Positive psychological changes and personal growth that occur after experiencing trauma or adversity.

Presence: Being fully engaged and attentive in the present moment, often involving mindfulness and focus.

Problem-Focused Coping: A type of stress management that targets the causes of stress through problem-solving and action.

Problem-Solving: The process of finding solutions to challenges or difficulties through analytical thinking and creativity.

Processing Emotions: The act of recognizing, understanding, and managing emotions, often involving reflection and self-awareness.

Psychological Flexibility: The ability to be in the present moment with full awareness and openness, guided by one's values.

Psychological Safety: A shared belief that a team or environment is safe for interpersonal risk-taking, promoting open communication and collaboration.

Rebuilding Trust: The process of restoring trust and confidence in a relationship after it has been broken or damaged.

Reconciliation: The act of resolving conflicts and restoring harmony in relationships, often through communication and forgiveness.

Recovery: The process of healing and returning to a state of well-being after experiencing physical, emotional, or mental challenges.

Reflected Appraisal: The process through which people come to understand themselves based on their perception of how others view them.

Reflection: Thoughtful consideration and contemplation of one's thoughts, experiences, and actions.

Regret: Feelings of sorrow or disappointment about past actions or decisions.

Rejection: The act of dismissing or excluding someone, often leading to feelings of hurt or inadequacy.

Resilience: The capacity to recover quickly from difficulties, challenges, or setbacks, demonstrating adaptability and strength.

Respect: Treating others with consideration, dignity, and regard for their feelings and rights.

Responsibility: Being accountable for one's actions and decisions, accepting the consequences of one's choices.

Restorative Justice: A method of conflict resolution that emphasizes repairing harm and promoting healing for all parties involved.

Rumination: The process of continuously thinking about the same thoughts, often negative or distressing, without finding a resolution.

Self-Awareness: The ability to recognize and understand one's emotions, strengths, weaknesses, and values.

Self-Compassion: Showing kindness, understanding, and empathy toward oneself, especially in times of difficulty or failure.

Self-Confidence: Trust in one's abilities, qualities, and judgment, leading to a positive self-image and assertiveness.

Self-Control: The ability to regulate and manage one's emotions, impulses, and behaviors in different situations.

Self-Disclosure: The process of revealing personal information about oneself to others, often to deepen interpersonal connections.

Self-Doubt: A lack of confidence in one's abilities or decisions, often leading to feelings of uncertainty.

Self-Efficacy: Belief in one's ability to succeed in achieving an outcome or reaching a goal.

Self-Esteem: The overall evaluation of one's self-worth and value as a person.

Self-Expression: The act of conveying one's thoughts, emotions, and personality through various means, such as communication and art.

Self-Growth: The continuous process of personal development and improvement, often involving learning and self-reflection.

Self-Regulation: The ability to manage and control one's emotions and behavior in different situations.

Self-Worth: A sense of one's own value and importance as an individual, regardless of external judgments or comparisons.

Sensitivity: Awareness and responsiveness to one's own emotions and the feelings of others.

Shame: A powerful feeling of embarrassment, unworthiness, or inadequacy, often linked to perceived personal flaws or mistakes.

Social Intelligence: The ability to understand and navigate social interactions effectively, including empathy and communication skills.

Social Skills: The skills used to interact and communicate effectively with others, often involving empathy and conflict resolution.

Social Support: Emotional, instrumental, or informational assistance and comfort provided by others in times of need.

Solitude: A state of being alone and enjoying one's own company, often for relaxation and self-reflection.

Somatic Awareness: Consciousness of one's body, its functions, and sensations, often used to regulate emotions and manage stress.

Speaking Up: Assertively expressing one's thoughts, opinions, or concerns, especially in situations where it may be difficult or uncomfortable.

Steadfastness: The quality of being unwavering and resolute in pursuing goals and values.

Stress Management: The ability to cope with and reduce stress through adaptive strategies and self-care.

Subjective Well-Being: A person's cognitive and affective evaluations of their life, encompassing overall life satisfaction and happiness.

Support: Providing encouragement, assistance, and emotional comfort to others, often during challenging times.

Sympathy: Feelings of pity and sorrow for someone else's misfortune or suffering.

Taking Breaks: The practice of resting and recharging both physically and mentally to maintain well-being and productivity.

Teamwork: Collaborating and working together effectively with others to achieve common goals.

Tolerance: The acceptance and respect of individual differences, including beliefs, cultures, and perspectives.

Trauma: Physical, emotional, or psychological injury or shock caused by a distressing event or experience.

Trust: The belief in the reliability, honesty, and integrity of oneself or others.

Understanding: The ability to comprehend and empathize with others' thoughts, feelings, and perspectives.

Uniqueness: Recognizing and celebrating the individuality and distinctiveness of oneself and others.

Validation: Recognition or affirmation that a person's feelings or opinions are valid or worthwhile.

Vulnerability: The quality or state of being exposed to the possibility of being attacked or harmed, either physically or emotionally.

Wisdom: The knowledge, insight, and judgment gained through life experiences and reflection.

Work-Life Balance: The equilibrium between professional responsibilities and personal life, promoting well-being and satisfaction.

Workaholism: An excessive and compulsive preoccupation with work, often leading to neglect of personal and social aspects of life.

Supplemental Book Series

Published by Pradoic LLC

Emotional Intelligence Modeled:

Each book is a collection of short stories covering a comprehensive list of potentially contentious everyday scenarios most all of us encounter. Each story models how a well-chosen emotional intelligence approach greatly improves relationship outcomes. These books can be found at: https://mybook.to/Accessible_EI_Brewer

1. Accessible Emotional Intelligence for Work and Career Development

2. Accessible Emotional Intelligence for Personal Emotional Challenges & Growth

3. Accessible Emotional Intelligence for Personal Relationships & Wellness

4. Accessible Emotional Intelligence for Challenges in Parenting, Education, and Your Community

5. Accessible Emotional Intelligence for Special Life Situation Challenges